First 100 Days of Selling
A Practical Day-by-Day
Guide to Excel in the Sales
Profession

Written by
Jim Ryerson

Ryerson, James, 1959 –

Other books by Jim Ryerson:

First 100 Days of In-home Selling, The Secret of the One-Call Close

Selling by THE BOOK Today, Timeless Wisdom in a Referral-based World

A lot has changed since *First 100 Days of Selling* was originally published in 2006. However, the basic fundamentals of selling have not changed and, if anything, are now more important than ever.

If you're reading this book, it's either early in your first sales role or you have been in sales for some time and are looking to grow your skills.

Maybe you're thinking about pursuing a sales position and want to know what to expect. Whatever your situation customers have many more choices than ever before. It continues to get more difficult for customers to decide among all the options. Customers also have less time due to continued pressure on productivity and cost. As a result, numerous programs have emerged that promise sales success in challenging times. Many sales programs stress in-depth psychoanalytical approaches to the client contact. Others focus on using technology to create heavy traffic and multiple leads. Still others rely on clichéd slogans, recycled ideas, or unproven theories. However, these programs fail to take the most important factor into account: A person's decision to engage with us, and ultimately buy from us, is based on how they feel about us and our ability to meet their needs.

But here's the best news: you can learn behaviors and processes that will help people have a good feeling about you from the first minute they meet you. It's work and it takes practice, patience, and perseverance. And that's what this book is all about.

YOUR FORWARD WILL REPLACE THESE TWO PAGES

To Leadership:

Thanks again for the opportunity to discuss your event. Should you allow us to work with your organization YOU will have the opportunity to write the forward for this book!

Our goal is to help everyone in your organization who engages with clients improve their selling skills. At your event, we will define the *What, How* and *When* action items from this book and customize the techniques for your team during breakout sessions. We then back the learning up with short, hyper-focused videos on our mobile training APP, Shot Of Octane™. Following the event, your team hits the road with their customized copy of *First 100 Days of Selling*, including your personal call to action in the Forward, a burst of Octane from the presentation, best practices captured during breakouts and ongoing learning with Shot Of Octane™ videos on our mobile app.

YOUR FORWARD WILL REPLACE THESE TWO PAGES

As leader of your sales team, your personalized Forward will position the event and the initiative to grow the sales talent in your organization. This Forward, the one you are reading right now, will be replaced with your personal words to your team along with your signature or the signatures of your leadership team. We will work with you to tie your event theme and goals with our content.

On the cover of *First 100 Days of Selling*, we will put your logo and event theme. Ultimately, this book will mark the beginning of creating a sales culture within your entire organization. We feel so strongly about this initiative we will customize the content regardless of the number of team members in your organization.

See you at the finish line,

Jim Ryerson
Chief Acceleration Officer
Sales Octane, Inc.

Table of Contents

TABLE OF CONTENTS

SECTION 5: Appointments

Introduction: The Sales Continuum™ - The Art, Science and Discipline of Sales

What you are about to read is the result of many years of sales experience and analysis of the sales process. I guarantee that no matter what your situation, you will walk away with a solid, step-by-step roadmap to selling. It includes not only what I've learned, but also the best practices of the best salespeople across numerous products, services, and markets.

It's not just another book about a specific sales technique or a particular sales trick. It's much more. This book defines a complete process based on the realities of day-to-day, in-the-trenches selling. I call this process the Sales Continuum.

The Sales Continuum covers the art, science and discipline of sales. The art of selling involves understanding your strengths and leveraging them. It involves learning your areas for improvement and practicing until you minimize the negative impact of those areas. When you learn the material so well over a period of time, through discipline, it becomes second nature. You've heard people remark that a sales person has mastered the "Art of Selling." This simply means they have worked at making their sales approach appear like they have done it successfully for a long, long time.

The question is what have they worked at that makes them so good? The answer is the science of selling. Shortly after I began sharing the Sales Continuum with salespeople around the world I encountered a particularly difficult attendee. I was told that this sales professional was the top salesperson in his company for several years in a row and was also considered one of the top in his industry. This sales professional was also nearing retirement and was not excited about the prospect of someone much younger – namely me – training him in a discipline where he clearly excelled. He sat towards the back of the room with his arms folded across his chest, clearly a visual sign of his disinterest.

As the day went on, I noticed him becoming a bit more engaged, especially with those at his table. It wasn't until lunch that he came up and shared with me that he really enjoyed our approach. He went on to say that he had been very blessed in the sales profession but that he never realized the science behind what had made him so successful. The science of selling consists of the behavioral and psychological elements of influencing your customer. This does not mean to manipulate them as that will eventually lead you down a dead end.

Finally, the discipline of selling takes our stated initiative ("I want to be the best salesperson in my company") and converts it to measurable, quantifiable steps that you can follow in a disciplined manner. This becomes our real initiative! You may have great stated initiative. The question is – do you have the real initiative to accomplish those goals?

In each chapter there are items that represent the Art, the Science and the Discipline of selling. This will help you identify how the information should help you achieve your stated initiative to become the best in your profession.

The Sales Continuum starts with your first hello and handshake with a potential prospect. The process continues to the handshake that closes the sale – and beyond, because what follows the sale is just as important as what leads to it. That's why I call the program a "continuum". The steps are connected, and each step is dependent on the others.

There are six key sales activities in the Sales Continuum:

Networking: the process of expanding your network and finding prospects.

Prospecting: the process of qualifying the accounts to identify your opportunity.

Appointments: the process of creating value.

Proposals: the actual submission of a proposal to a prospect.

Closing: the point at which the client accepts your proposal and you have the order.

Referrals: a referral from an existing client

We'll go in-depth with each of these steps later.

An important part of the Sales Continuum process is my LINK program, which was developed to give you a framework and repeatable process for successful networking. Each letter in the word LINK stands for something you need to know about everyone you meet: Line (of work), Interests, Needs, and Knowledge.

I feel this approach is ideal for the sales environment we are entering, where prospects will continue to get harder to reach. At the same time prospects are being bombarded with more and more products and services *just like yours*. How will they make a decision to take your call? How will they decide to choose your product or service over the mass of competitors making their own pitches? The answer: The Sales Continuum.

This program is a complete, comprehensive approach to sales that deals with every aspect of the sales process: Networking, Prospecting, Qualifying, Appointment, Trial Closing/Closing and Referral.

These are the activities sales professionals do every day, and it's the process we teach. If you're looking for a trick, this is not for you. If you are going to invest in selling as a career, then this is the ideal process to build a business that will continue to grow and fuel future growth. Like other sales programs, the key is creating a stream of referrals. But the Sales Continuum does it differently. We create referrals at every step of the sales process.

One last thought: for years I thought that the top sales performers were fortunate and just happened to stumble into the right situation at the right time. Once I realized that top sales performers had a specific approach to creating their success, I set my focus on understanding that process and defining the details that drive it.

See you at the finish line!

Jim Ryerson

Getting Started: Think Outside the Funnel

Most salespeople are familiar with the idea of the sales funnel.

Sales Funnel

The funnel is filled with "suspects"—people you suspect are candidates for your products or services. We research and/or follow up with these suspects in a "prospecting" phase, much like the prospectors who searched for gold. Our goal is to prospect and ultimately connect with them so we can move to the next step: qualification.

Through various questions, data gathering, and plain observation we determine if they are, in fact, qualified as a candidate for our products or services. If they are, the lead moves down the funnel. The funnel gets narrower since many of your suspects never materialize as qualified leads. For leads that move farther down the funnel, you work to uncover their needs and identify all the reasons why they would benefit from your product or service.

After finding a qualified prospect you connect the features, advantages, and benefits of your product/service with the prospect's needs. If the prospect is still interested, you provide them with a proposal and then close after you deal with any objections they have. The bottom of the funnel is where you close and either win or lose the sale.

Incidentally, "close" may mean you get the order, or it may mean you "close" the file because you have lost. It could also mean nothing will happen until the future, if at all. Whether you win or lose does not change the fact that the customer exits the bottom of the funnel.

Whenever I hear salespeople talk about the funnel, they say they work every stage of the funnel but feel guilty when they focus on anything other than what is "inside the funnel." However, our experience suggests that a great deal of a salesperson's time is spent "below the funnel," making sure the implementation occurred correctly after the sale. Regardless of your business, whatever occurs after you close a sale is referred to as implementation.

The company you work for may have people deployed against the implementation process, but you may have to drive many of the implementation issues. Even though we are not directly involved in the process of implementation we take accountability to make certain the implementation goes as planned.

When I ask successful salespeople why they get involved with implementation issues, they say they learn a great deal about their customer during the implementation stage. They learn whether the solutions they promised in their proposals are accurate. They get firsthand confirmation of the issues, often referred to as the client's "pain," that they addressed in their proposal. They learn about other problems that their product/service can solve. They often gain a better idea of the value/savings their customers experience with their product/service.

On top of all that, the relationship the salesperson creates with the client during the implementation phase becomes stronger because the salesperson is present whenever there are issues and takes total accountability for satisfying the customer. But if you look at the typical sales funnel, it's not a salesperson's job to be accountable during the implementation phase. And that's where the traditional sales funnel process has to change.

In the real world, it is essential for the sales process to recognize that performance during the implementation phase is part of a salesperson's accountability in the eyes of the customer. Of course, the goal of a leader/sales manager is to provide the necessary support and follow-through to minimize the amount of time a salesperson has to spend on implementation. Nevertheless, the salesperson must always be accountable because it positions them for the next and most important step of the sales process.

Getting Referrals

Let me ask you if this is your personal buying experience. When I've ever acquired a product that did not work as well as I was told it would work it was because:

1. The product did not do what was promised, or

2. I did not get good follow-through by the company on how to use it, or

3. I'm an idiot and was not using it properly.

Whatever the reason, I was dissatisfied and would typically try to connect back with the salesperson who sold me the product/ service. They were often unavailable or inattentive to deal with my dissatisfaction. Often their lack of availability or inattention to my needs was not just confined to the implementation process. It was just the way they did business. And guess how I felt when I came to that conclusion?

After repeated attempts to find a solution, I would toss the product aside and look for another solution and, share my dissatisfaction with people I know — the company's other prospective customers. However, when I acquired a product/service that did not work but the salesperson was available and willing to do everything possible to make sure the problem was solved, I would rave about the product/service to others. Even when I acquire a product/service that works as promised, I find that the salespeople who stay in touch with me better position themselves for my next acquisition.

You have to take the time, initiative and accountability to make certain the product/service performs the way your customer expects "below the funnel." It is non-negotiable. When you make sure they are totally satisfied, you'll get additional business from them. And far more important: you will get a chance to ask for referrals. If you make certain they are satisfied, you earn the right to ask for referrals.

We hear a lot about the topic of referrals, but most salespeople see referrals as reactive versus proactive. A salesperson is pleased when they receive a call from a prospect who was referred by an existing customer. That's easy. What we are talking about is proactively working to develop a referral stream.

There are two important reasons why we want to proactively develop referrals. First, the sales cycle is shorter when a referral is involved. Prospecting a referral requires fewer prospecting calls. Getting the prospect's attention and differentiating your product/service from all the other options on the market takes far less time. Second, you will close at a higher rate when a referral is involved.

Unfortunately, most salespeople don't make the connection between how they can speed up their sales cycle and improve their closing percentage. This is one of the key outcomes of the Sales Continuum process. You will position yourself for the referral, which will speed up your sales cycle and improve your closing percentage. In addition, you will assume 100 percent accountability, because at a minimum you must meet your customer's expectations in order to reasonably expect to receive a referral. This is a key trait of top sales professionals. They assume total accountability because they recognize they lose the opportunity for referrals *if* the customer's expectations are not met.

When a salesperson structures their entire sales process by focusing on obtaining referrals they will find they are standing on a field of gold. The Sales Continuum will help you prospect for that gold.

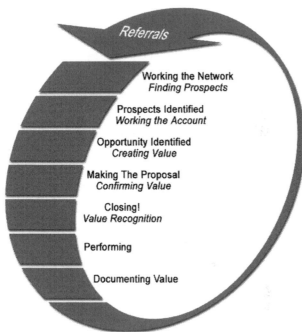

The Sales Continuum™

How to Use This Book

To gain the most benefits from this book, read one chapter a day. The book is set up to begin on a Monday (Day 1) and continues for five days, Monday through Friday, with the step-by-step approach of the Sales Continuum. The subsequent two days (Days 6 and 7) are specific guiding principles for sales professionals and will revive, renew and inspire you on your weekend. The weekend days are called Sales Octane Mantras. The balance of the book follows the same five days of sales process and two days of inspiration. Each day you will learn the material, do some exercises, and develop positive selling habits. It won't take long. Best of all, you'll have the foundation and the framework for a successful and rewarding career in sales.

It's a great way to start the day!

SECTION 1: Knowing Yourself and Influencing Others

DAY 1
Preparation: Get Going Early! Read, Plan, and Restore

Sales is one of the most rewarding careers due to the opportunities and independence it provides. Sales is one of the highest paid professions and offers greater independence than any other occupation.

The rewards, income, and independence all begin with a quick start. Your clients and prospective clients are typically available early and late in the day. If you get going early you will have the opportunity to talk to more clients than your competition. Decide what "early" is for you and set a goal to meet that expectation each and every day. Take your planner, PDA, or electronic calendar and mark it in every morning!

Take a few minutes of this early time to read this book, plan and restore. Reading is one of the key differentiators between those who accomplish great things and those who don't. The average person reads less than two books per year. Your commitment to reading this book places you ahead of the pack!

Briefly scan Days 9 through 11 today so you begin to think about where you can locate the information. This will give you a glimpse at how much farther you will be within days and help you balance your week with other activities that your company requires. Keep in mind that this discipline of starting early and beginning with reading should be a life-long habit. In 100 days you'll be completely done with this book. Then find another book on sales and read that during your early hours. You can download my "Recommended Reading" list free at *www.salesoctane.com*. We frequently add books to the list so you may want to pencil this activity in your planner every few months to check the list.

Plan

You'll learn more about planning later on. However, for the duration of this book, review the goals of each day to make sure you accomplish the tasks in this book. They are the most important steps to ensuring success so place them at the top of the list!

Restore

Whatever the foundation in your life, I recommend taking a few minutes of this early morning ritual to reflect on that foundation. This adds perspective to the day and gives you the strength you will need when you encounter obstacles.

Move ahead

Now that you have read the Forward, Introduction, Getting Started, How to Use this Book and Day 1, continue with your existing sales activities. If selling is what you're meant to do you are going to have the time of your life.

Enjoy!

DAY 2
Know Yourself – It Starts with You: Part I

People buy from people they like. If you are buying a candy bar at the local convenience store you probably don't care if you like the person behind the counter. You buy the candy bar and move on. However, when someone has a choice of who to buy from or when they have to deal with a salesperson for a period of time they will buy from someone they like versus someone they dislike. This makes sense and most salespeople understand this concept and work diligently at being friendly and liked by their customers. However, your potential customer is also more inclined to buy from someone who is similar to them. We refer to this similarity as their behavioral style. You have a particular behavioral style and your potential customer has a particular behavioral style. The way they make their decisions is influenced by their behavioral style. For the next several days we will be touching on the concept of how a prospect makes decisions and how we can modify our approach to make it easier for them to buy from us versus our competitor. We are talking about how the prospect processes information in their mind when making a decision, how they behave. Think about it this way. When I decide to buy something, I am quite impulsive. I recently bought a car over the Internet. After looking for a particular model on the Internet I found a few cars matching my criteria. Those particular cars were selling fast and when I called about the first two they were sold within the next twenty-four hours. As a result I bought the third car that met my criteria, over the phone, with a simple deposit on my credit card without having viewed the car in person or driven the vehicle. The car was in another city so I purchased a one-way plane ticket to the city where it was located and drove it home.

Some of you are aghast at the thought of making a sizeable purchase without doing a lot of research. Many of you would review information online about the model you were looking to purchase, go to several automobile dealerships, evaluate several vehicles, drive them, look at the history of the car, etc., etc. Some may even think it's reckless to make a major purchase in this manner. And that's the point. It was not reckless for me but it is for others. People think about buying decisions differently and in some cases very differently. Unfortunately, many salespeople never realize the way *they* make buying decisions is often different from how a prospect will make a buying decision. Issues such as the amount of information or analysis required, their level of suspicion or trust, their impulsiveness or lack thereof, how quickly they make a decision and their level of emotional engagement in a purchase are just a few of the ways that people differ in how they make decisions. The unknowing salesperson will approach every prospect with the same type of information, the same quantity of information, the same "lines," the same follow-up and the same close. With some prospects they win and with some prospects they lose. You could get more business, faster, at higher margins *and* position yourself better for the referral *by understanding* how the prospect makes decisions from a behavioral standpoint and then adapting your approach to fit their style!

Incidentally, if you are asking yourself the question, "Jim, how often is the behavioral style of the prospect different from my behavioral style?" It can be as high as 75 percent of the time! That means you may only have a 25 percent chance the prospect behaves just like you when making a decision. Those are not good odds.

The goal of these next few days is to understand your behavioral style and how *you* come across to your prospects and customers and then how to identify your prospects behavioral style. We will give you a general approach to adapting your approach on Days 6 through 8, and then later in the book (Days 61 on) we go into greater detail with how to prepare for each style, what to do during the sales call with each style and how to follow up after the sales call with each style. In some cases the approach will be very different from the way you currently "sell" and in some cases it will be similar. However, before we look at the prospect's style and how to approach them we want to make sure *you* know your behavioral style. Our organization uses a tool available through Target Training International. You can get more information at our website *www.salesoctane.com*. There are two options to help you identify your sales behavioral style.

1. You can take an online assessment by visiting our website *www.salesoctane.com*. This online assessment will not only provide you with your exact behavioral style but it will also give you twenty-plus pages of insight into how you present yourself to others, how you respond to stress when selling, how you adapt yourself and a review of your strengths and areas for improvement as a salesperson.

2. You can go to Day 3 and follow the same methodology we use to identify a prospect's behavioral style.

Note: Three important reminders if you take the online assessment:

1) This will require ten to fifteen minutes of uninterrupted time (once you start please make sure you finish the assessment in a single sitting).

2) Answer the questions as you *are* and *not how you wish you could be* or not how your manager would want you to answer. If you answer honestly you will have a very clear indication of how to improve your approach to get additional business. The only style that is bad for selling is the one you don't know (see Sales Octane Mantra #3 on Day 13).

3) Once you complete the assessment online you will *immediately* receive a copy of the results! Please have someone that has known you for some time read the overview of your results (typically the first two to four pages) and ask them the following question: "How accurate do you think this is?"

Oftentimes you may feel like it is 80 percent accurate but someone close to you will say it's 95 to 100 percent accurate! Be prepared to learn! If you have taken the assessment online through *www.salesoctane.com* please proceed to Day 4.

DAY 3
Know Yourself: Part II

The four behavioral styles from a sales perspective

If you have taken the assessment this is a review of the information. If you have not taken the assessment then identify your style from the simple steps below which is similar to how you will identify the style of a prospect or customer. The reason we feel strongly you should take the assessment online is that most people are a blend of two or more styles and the online assessment reconciles that blending of multiple styles giving you a more accurate view of your behavioral style.

There are four behavioral styles:

> 1. D = Dominant/Driver
>
> 2. I = Influencer/Expressive
>
> 3. S = Steady/Steadiness
>
> 4. C = Compliant/Analytical

While most people are a blend of behavioral styles we are going to review the individual styles as if the person were 100 percent Dominant/Driver, Influencer/Expressive, Steady/Steadiness or Compliant/Analytical. Answer these two questions:

Question 1 – Are you an Extrovert or an Introvert? If you are not sure then ask someone else what they think you are.

Question 2 – Are you more task and detail oriented or are you more people oriented?

Again, if you are not sure then ask someone else what they think you are.

Now, based on the answers to these two questions you can arrive at a reasonable indication of your dominant behavioral style. Here's how the responses lead to your style.

Compliant	Driver	Task & Detail-Oriented
Steady	Influencer	People-Oriented
Introverts	Extroverts	

Table 1 – Behavioral Styles

If you are Extroverted and task and detail oriented you have a Dominant/Driver behavioral style. If you are Extroverted and people-oriented you have an Influencer behavioral style. If you are Introverted and task and detail oriented you have a Compliant behavioral style. If you are Introverted and people oriented you have a Steady behavioral style.

Note: This simple two-question approach does not take into consideration the blending of two or more styles. Therefore, the list of how each style approaches decisions may change depending on your unique style. The online assessment recognizes the blending and provides a more accurate and complete list of your unique characteristics.

The following list is how each behavioral style makes decisions:

Dominant/Driver makes decisions – decisively, impatiently, responsibly, taking calculated risk, competitively.

Influencer/Expressive makes decisions – impulsively, the popular choice, emotional, trusting, enthusiastically.

Steady/Steadiness makes decisions – consistently (with past decisions), patiently, with little emotion, deliberately, safely.

Compliant/Analytical makes decisions – cautiously, carefully, exacting, detailed, systematically.

Identify your behavioral style(s) and move to the next day.

Note: Many of the behavioral characteristics and adaptations noted in the book are taken from work done by Target Training International © 2005 - 2013 Target Training International.

DAY 4
How Do You Identify the Prospect's Behavioral Style?

Now that you know your style we want to look at how to identify the style of the person sitting across from you or the person on the other end of the phone. Because you can't have a person take an assessment you have to identify their dominant style from several observations. These observations can be made over the phone and face to face. Clearly, being face to face will provide much greater insight into their behavioral style but you can pick up many clues over the phone and even from their voice mail message.

There are two questions you must ask/observe and these become the basis for determining their behavioral style. The first observation you must make is whether the person is an Extrovert or an Introvert (see Table 1 from Day 3). Here are the words that define these two behaviors. Extroverts are outgoing, gregarious, enthusiastic, talkative, assertive, social, outgoing, and active. Introverts are low key, deliberate, less emotional, quiet, shy, reserved and contemplative. This is typically the easier of the two observations you must make. Take a look at the list of characteristics and think of your fellow workers, friends and relatives. Can you separate the Extroverts from the Introverts? The second observation you must make is whether the person is task and detail oriented or whether they are people oriented (Table 1).Here are the words that define these two behaviors. Those who are task and detail oriented are busy, analytical, questioning, detailed, thoughtful, and organized. Those who are people oriented are friendly, cooperative, warm, agreeable and sociable. This is typically the most difficult of the two observations you must make. Take a look at the list of characteristics and think of your fellow workers, friends and relatives. Can you separate those who are task and detail oriented from those who are people oriented? Now think about your prospect!

Whether you are on the phone or face to face you can hear or observe many of these traits. For today, make several phone calls to ice-cold prospects, particularly those that you really never anticipate getting business from or even qualifying as an opportunity (translation: who cares what happens on these phone calls!). Listen to the way they talk. Listen to their voice mail greeting. How much detail do they leave in their greeting? How much emotion do you hear in their greeting? When you get someone on the phone how much emotion do they show? How do they ask questions and how much information do they want? Are they looking for a lot of detail? Do they sound optimistic or pessimistic? Are they pushy and impatient?

Next, if/when you are face to face, look for these signs that will give you a good indication:

- Dominant/Driver – Status office (prestigious committee/award plaques on wall), a lot going on, initiate conversations, blunt/direct.

- Influencer – Office with "experience" pictures (skiing, hiking, golfing, group/team pictures), emotional, spontaneous, piles of work (less organization), demonstrative (busy and animated gestures), optimistic.

- Steady – Relaxed, cooperative, office with more family pictures, modest, patient.

- Compliant – Office with graphs, charts & details, quieter, questioning, perfectionist, distrustful, pessimistic.

Watch for these characteristics in others you meet on sales calls or hear over the phone. Begin to write down their behavioral style wherever you keep information about your contacts so you can use the techniques you learn during the following days.

DAY 5
Manage Your Expectations

Confidence is a major contributor to sales success. All other issues being equal the sales professional with confidence will outperform the salesperson that lacks confidence. One of the ways to improve your confidence is by managing your expectations based on your fit with the style of your prospect or customer. Some styles are complimentary in the sales process and others are not. Once you finish today's material you will no doubt recall a time when you struggled with a prospect or customer. When you look at the table included in this day, you may find that their style was either a poor or fair match with your style. Those situations often erode our self-confidence and have a negative impact on subsequent sales calls.

By managing our expectations going into the sales situation we can keep our self-confidence intact. The process works like this. First, locate your dominant style as the *salesperson* on the table placed at the end of this day. Next, identify the style of your customer along the top of the table. Let's say you are an Influencer, like me. (If you have a blend of more than one you can take your other dominant styles into consideration.) Based on the table, if I am selling to another Influencer I have a *good* match and there's a *good* chance of a successful call. If I am selling to a Driver I also have a good chance. But when it comes to the Steady I only have a *fair* chance and with the Compliant I have a *poor* chance. This is very important for me to know! When I find myself in a selling situation where the customer has a Compliant style I need to recognize that I will have to adapt in a number of ways. Those "adaptations" may feel very unnatural or against my normal approach to selling and typically does not feel as good as when I am selling to a Driver or Influencer. By recognizing this fact, I can manage my expectations for the call and not allow it to substantially impact my self-confidence. For today, recall several recent sales calls that have gone well and several sales calls that were a challenge. Try to remember each customer and identify their behavioral style from Day 4. Using the table in this day, see how often the calls that have gone well were because the customer had a good or excellent match and how often the calls that were a challenge were because the customer was either a *poor* or *fair* match. By managing your expectations you will maintain your self-confidence which is critical to a sales professional.

CUSTOMER

	STYLE	DRIVER	INFLUENCER	STEADY	COMPLIANT
S **A** **L** **E** **S** **P** **E** **R** **S** **O** **N**	DRIVER	GOOD	GOOD	FAIR	POOR
	INFLUENCER	GOOD	GOOD	FAIR	POOR
	STEADY	FAIR	GOOD	EXCELLENT	EXCELLENT
	COMPLIANT	POOR	POOR	EXCELLENT	EXCELLENT

DAY 6
Sales Octane Mantra #1—The Golden Rule of Selling Should Be, "Do unto others as they would like"

We've all heard the golden rule "Do unto others as you would have them do unto you." And while this is very sensible and I recommend you follow this rule there is an additional rule that will help you as a sales professional. From a selling perspective, if I "do unto others" as I would have them "do unto me" it assumes they make buying decisions the same way I would. I am assuming they want the same amount of detail, the same social approach, the same amount of contact, the same pressure, the same everything. And that's not accurate. There are many different types of people out there with different behavioral styles and different ways of making decisions. By approaching them the way I want to be approached I am rolling the dice that this is the way they want to be approached. They will feel like they are being "sold." The next time you are tempted to use the same approach with every customer, remember Sales Octane Mantra #1 "Do unto others as they would like."

DAY 7
Sales Octane Mantra #2—People Love to Buy but They Hate to Be Sold!

Sales professionals understand and embrace this principle. They work hard to create a selling environment where the prospect feels free to make a buying decision. They work hard to minimize the pressure that causes a prospect to feel like they may be making a hasty decision. In short, sales professionals work hard to influence the prospect to buy while eliminating the pressure associated with being sold.

There are five techniques you can use to minimize pressure and let the prospect buy.

* Approach each sales opportunity like you don't need the sale. Sales professionals know that a prospect can sense their desperation. If you go into a sales opportunity by telling yourself "I have to get this sale," you are desperate. You will try too hard and the prospect will feel like they are being sold. Instead, go into each sales opportunity by telling yourself you don't need the sale. This will cause *you* to appear less desperate and the *prospect* will become more comfortable and less suspicious of your motives.

* Ask questions. That's right, when you ask questions the prospect talks more and you talk less. The less you talk the less chance you have to come off as a high-pressure sales person. The less you talk the better the chance the prospect will share what they are looking for and why they want to buy.

- Believe that your product or service will have a positive impact on your prospect. Your prospect will pick up on your confidence in your product and that will make them more comfortable. You may have to invest more time in the short term to learn about your product so you can have that confidence!

- Make more calls after you complete a sale. Success breeds success.

- Learn how to adapt to their style. Commit to memory the techniques beginning with Day 61 so you know how to adapt and when to close.

Become a sales professional. Minimize pressure and increase the comfort of the buying experience. Your customers will *LOVE* to buy from you!

DAY 8
Mirror the Basics

On a very basic level your prospect is more comfortable with someone who is similar or "like" them versus someone who is dissimilar or "unlike" them. Think about your own preferences. If you are someone who talks rapidly and with passion about a topic you are more comfortable when the person sitting across from you speaks with passion and at an accelerated rate. If you are someone who contemplates their words carefully and shows little emotion when discussing a topic you will be suspicious if the person sitting across from you speaks rapidly and with passion! It's just the way we are.

In the selling arena you should use this information to make your clients feel more comfortable with you. Once you recognize the prospect's rate of speech, their tone and their level of emotion you should adapt when you speak to them. This will make your prospect more comfortable with you and that will only benefit both parties. It's a win – win situation!

For today, identify your rate of speech, tone and level of emotion. Practice doing the opposite. Then look for someone who is unlike you and try to modify your approach. See how it feels. Keep track of how comfortable they appear to become by how long the conversation lasts and the amount of information they share.

DAY 9
Gather Things Together: Starting With What You Have

In the book *Acres Of Diamonds* by Russell H. Conwell, the main character sold his land to go in search of diamonds. Little did he know that the land he lived on was found to be the richest diamond field in recent history.

The same can be said of your new opportunity. Most new sales professionals take over for a previous salesperson. There's a tendency to want to start fresh, hit the road and go in search of riches. However, there are most likely some great contacts right in your backyard. As a result, it's essential that you focus on these high payoff opportunities!

The following is a list of materials to gather today:

• Get a complete list of everyone your company has ever done business with, including current clients for your territory.

• Find out if your predecessor had a list of prospects they had contacted or sent marketing materials.

• Look for open proposals regardless of when they were submitted or whether your predecessor/company had followed up.

• Identify a list of top prospects with which you want to do business in the future.

Take all this information and compile it into the following four categories:

Existing Clients

If you have an account base given to you when you start, or if you've spent several years in sales, keep a single list of existing accounts that continue to purchase your products or services on a regular basis. Label this group **Clients.** We always want to be able to view this list with minimal effort. We're going to break this down in the future but a single list is perfect for today.

Open Proposals

Create a single list of all the current proposals for prospective or existing customers. Label this group **Open Proposals.**

Past Customers

Create a list of anyone who has used your company's product/services in the past that are *not* using your product/services today. Even if you just lost them last week, put it on this list labeled **Past Customers.**

"Wish List" Opportunities (The Wish 100)

What companies, individuals or organizations do you want to be doing business with in the future? Make a list of these prospective accounts regardless of the challenges associated with penetrating them. Don't over think this step. Simply write down the names of the prospective companies, individuals, or organizations. In the future, as you hear about new candidates for the Wish List simply add them! We'll discuss how to use this list to develop networking opportunities with key decision makers and how to position yourself for a sales opportunity.

This visual list of consolidated opportunities will serve three purposes going forward.

1. It will be a constant reminder of the tremendous opportunity you have. As you convert prospects to customers and customers to clients your list will continue to grow.

2. As the list grows it will be a positive reinforcement of your sales ability. This positive reinforcement will help you overcome challenges and obstacles.

3. As you meet people, read the Internet newspaper and industry articles, you will see names from your list of opportunities. You can use this knowledge to re-connect with clients or reach out to prospects on your list

Don't be afraid to delegate. Many of these Day 9 activities can be delegated to others if you have a team. Share with them the goal of this book and your determination to stay on track. Ask for their help and show them how they fit into the puzzle. Have *them* read the book and ask "How do you think *we* can accomplish this together?" And, "What other ideas can you think of that are not in the book?"

By the way, I'd like to hear them. Send me your ideas in email to *jim@salesoctane.com*. We will send you a personalized coffee mug if we use the idea in our next book.

Go have some fun. Tomorrow you begin the single most important activity to generate sales. This can be a lot of work and will demand your persistence. Rest up.

DAY 10
Start Every Day by Closing Sales and Open the Door to Opportunity

Why would we start the day by closing open proposals? Because you can't expect to close business unless you tenaciously follow upon the proposals you have on the street. The longer these open proposals remain on the street, the probability increases that you won't get the sale. This won't require much time and certainly not much planning once you get going. Regardless of what sales system you use, you must have a clear line of sight to your open proposals.

Note: If you are a new salesperson, you may have been given some open proposals from your predecessors. It is essential that you follow up on these warm opportunities as soon as possible.

When you start the day calling on those proposals, you tell the prospective customers three things about yourself:

1. You are organized. You have a process and follow it...something they wish they were doing!

2. You are persistent. You will do whatever it takes to get the job done...something they are hoping to find in a sales person. You are already beginning to plant the seed in their mind that you will do what you say you're going to do!

3. You are committed to following through...something they hope to find in a salesperson.

By telling them you will call back on a certain day to follow upon the open proposal, you are telling them what you're going to do. Then by following up on that specific day, you are doing what you said you were going to do. While this may seem obvious, it's important, because most salespeople (not sales professionals) get caught in the "try trap." That is, "I'll try to call you tomorrow." "I'll try to connect with you next week." "I'll try to stop by later." Sales professionals use different language. They say what they are going to do and then *do it!*

If you don't have any open proposals, the concept is essential to successful selling so don't skip past Day 10 until you've embraced this concept. Remember, each and every day of your selling career from now on, you will begin the day by closing. And since you can only close business which has been proposed, you'll need to take your list of open proposals and make the calls! There are a number of reasons we put off making the follow-up calls. If you catch yourself saying anything similar to the following four statements you need to avoid going into denial. Make the call!

1. **"They didn't call back so they must not be interested"**

   This is a common thought that goes through the mind of a salesperson. And once you don't make the call for several days you begin to feel guilty that you didn't follow up so you procrastinate longer. The next thing you know the proposal is so old you're embarrassed to call.

2. **"I know what the answer is going to be...just a bunch of objections and rejection."**

   This is the type of negative self-talk that increases fear and diminishes your positive energy. The best way to overcome fear is to plunge directly into the thing you fear.

3. **"I have so much to do; I'll make the call later."**

   Salespeople are paid to sell, and everything else is busywork.

4. **"I don't want to appear to be a pest by leaving a message every day."**

   You're not a pest. You're showing just how organized, efficient, and effective you're going to be should they entrust their business to you. If you're this tenacious about one order, just think how great you will be when you get their business!

Script 1 – for voice mail message if potential customer does not answer the phone:

"Hello, this is John Smith from Acme Medical. I'm looking at our proposal dated MM/DD/YY, for (product). I want to follow up and find out if we provided you with all the information you need. I'll call back tomorrow morning, or, if you have a moment, feel free to call me at **444-444-4444**. Again, **444-444-4444**. Have a great day."

Script 2 – for the following day and subsequent messages:

"Hello, this is John Smith from Acme Medical. I'm sorry I missed you. I left a message regarding our proposal to you dated MM/DD/YY, for (product)." (Adjust the following to fit your situation.) "I'm going to be out with several clients for the rest of this week, but I'll give *you* a call next Monday to follow up and find out if you have any questions or need any additional information. My number is **444-444-4444**. Again, John at **444-444-4444**. Have a great day."

A word of encouragement and caution: as time progresses you will find that you made call after call after call to some prospective customers. My experience has been that these difficult customers became the most loyal clients after I secured their trust in my product/service. If you look at each unreturned call as simply a step toward the inevitable sale, you'll approach the calls more positively.

This is where the caution comes in. Too often a salesperson lets anxiety and disgust develop because the prospect has not returned numerous calls. Soon, their voice begins to send a clear message of anger that they are continuing to leave voice messages without so much as a return message.

You'll be glad you made the calls! Now write the script in your own words and start making the calls…every day from now on!

DAY 11
Set Goals and See Where You're Going

This is not a general goal-setting exercise. This is a sales activity goal-setting exercise. The same way a successful business has a budget with specific goals, you too will generate improved and predictable results by "budgeting" for the six key sales results you will generate when you use the Sales Continuum:

Networking: the process of expanding your network and finding prospects.

Prospecting: the process of qualifying the accounts to identify your opportunity.

Appointments: the process of creating value.

Proposals: the actual submission of a proposal to a prospect.

Closing: the point at which the client accepts your proposal and you have the order.

Referrals: a referral from an existing client or someone in your network.

This is a very specific exercise that identifies daily targets for these sales activities that ultimately drive sales volume. By maintaining a balance between these steps you will find your sales volume and opportunities increase.

Step 1. Start with the result you want

What do you want to earn? What is your income goal? If you are a self-employed entrepreneur, write down your sales volume goal and proceed to Step 3.

Step 2. Convert to a Sales Volume

Most sales positions have a variable component in the form of commission/sales bonus. Take your commission plan and calculate what sales volume you must accomplish to achieve your income goal.

Hint: If you are totally lost with your compensation plan, simply ask your sales manager "How do I make (insert your Annual Income Goal here) with our current compensation plan?" Then, as he or she explains the plan make certain you end up with a specific Sales Volume Goal.

Step 3. Average order size

It is essential that you determine the average order size for the products/services you sell. Remember, this is an average. Ask your manager or, if self-employed, look at your sales volume over a short period of time and then divide it by the number of orders. The result is your average order size.

Note: Projecting a lower average order size is beneficial because a lower average order size will set a higher goal and help you exceed your expectations.

Step 4. Calculating your annual, weekly and daily orders, sales and transactions goal

Take the sales volume goal from Step 2 and divide it by the average order size from Step 3. The result is the number of orders/sales/transactions you need to process each year. Divide it by the number of weeks you plan to work in a year and you have your weekly order/sales/transactions goal. Divide it by the number of days in a week you plan to work and you have a daily order/sales transaction goal. If you are using the spreadsheet from our website these calculations are completed automatically.

Step 5. Average close rate

The average close rate reflects how many orders you receive relative to the proposals you submit. If you submit ten proposals and close one sale from those proposals, then you have a 10 percent close rate (1/10 = .10 or 10 percent). If you submit fifteen proposals and close five sales from those proposals then you have a 33percent close rate (5/15 = .33 or 33 percent). If you do not have any detail to complete this closing percentage calculation then ask someone from your office or industry for their typical closing percentage.

Step 6. Proposal Goal

Take your annual/weekly/daily order goal from Step 4 and multiply it by your average close rate percentage. The result is the number of proposals you will need to submit on a annual/weekly/daily basis.

Step 7. Appointment/call Ratio

This next step involves setting specific quantitative appointment or phone contact goals depending on whether your specific sale involves phone-to-phone selling or face-to-face selling. This is something that will take some experience to develop, however, you can ask someone with sales experience at your company or in your industry how many face-to-face appointments or phone-to-phone contacts it takes before you get the opportunity to present a proposal.

Step 8. Calculating your Appointment/Call goal

Once you identify the ratio of appointments/calls to sales(example 3:1) simply take the percentage (example 1/3 = 33%)and divide your proposal goal from Step 6 by the percentage from Step 7 and the end result is the number of appointments/calls you need to have per year. You can then create a monthly and weekly appointment/calls goal.

Step 9. Contacts Goal

The last step in the process is how many people (contacts) you need to meet in order to meet your sales goal. This is not a scientific number. One of the primary factors in successful selling is meeting other people. The more people you know the more opportunity you have. As we like to say, as you increase your network, you increase your net worth!

For Step 9 you are simply going to pick the number of new people (contacts) you will meet *and put into your contact database* every week, month and year. Pick a number!

Congratulations, you know where you're going! A journey of a thousand miles begins with the first step. Every great result begins with several much smaller intentional activities. So write down your goals in every space you occupy while selling: office, home office, car, laptop, and desktop — everywhere.

Before you get too concerned about all these goals stop and think about what you've accomplished. With this minimal investment of time you have a clear goal of the number of proposals you need to submit and close in order to exceed your income goal. Those first two steps will give you greater focus as you proceed in your sales career. Many salespeople begin with the greatest intentions, but because they did not develop the daily and weekly plans around these key sales activities they never achieve their goals.

DAY 12
Sales Octane Mantra #3—Ignorance Is Not Bliss. Ignorance Is Ignorance

Ignorance is not knowing what to do to get started. Ignorance is not having a plan. Ignorance is not knowing what to do next once you get started. Ignorance is *not* bliss. You remember the 80-20 rule, also known as the Pareto principle. Applied to salespeople you can project that 80 percent of the salespeople will split 20 percent of the commissions while the remaining 20 percent of the salespeople—what we call sales professionals—will split 80 percent of the commissions. Think about it: very few people split a huge pie in one room, while in another room a lot of salespeople fight for a very, very small pie. Which do you want to be? Not the ignorant ones! This 100 day approach is hard work but it's intended to position you in a very elite group of sales professionals and help you achieve your financial goals.

DAY 13
Sales Octane Mantra #4—Dimes for a Dollar? The "Worth" Exercise

As you begin this journey of sales you will find there will be no shortage of people, problems, opportunities, and tasks begging for your time and attention. One of the ways to stay focused is to recognize the incredible value of every minute of your time. This exercise will help you make better decisions when someone or something begins to beg for your time, or worse, you procrastinate and start to lose valuable minutes.

Follow these six steps and make sure to complete all six steps today.

Step 1. Write down how much you want to make this next twelve months. Don't aim low! What would you need to make in order to feel fulfilled and content in your role? We'll use an example of $187,500.

Step 2. Identify how many days you will work. There are fifty-two weeks a year and seven days a week for and the average salesperson has thirteen holidays and fifteen days of vacation. Add your holidays and vacation days up and subtract the number from 364.

Example: 13 holidays and 15 days of vacation equals 28 – 365 =337 days to earn your goal from Step 1.

Step 3. Protect your personal time. The sales professional is one of the most highly pressured roles where you are "on-call" and thinking about business at all times, day and night. As a result you need to take time to restore your energy in order to stay in top form. The weekends are typically the time when we re-invest in ourselves. It's important to protect that personal time; therefore, for the purposes of this exercise we recommend protecting two days a week.

Two days per week times fifty-two weeks a year equals 104days of personal time. If you want to modify that amount because you plan to work less or more days per week simply modify the amount and subtract it from the result in Step 2.

Example: 2 days per week times 52 weeks a year equals 104 days minus 337 (from Step 2) equals 233 available days to earn your goal from Step 1.

Step 4. Stay focused. According to the Bureau of Labor Statistics the average workday is 8.335 hours. Since this is an average you will have to decide on your own number. Take the number of hours per day you will remain a focused sales professional and multiply that number by the number of days from Step 3.

Example: 8.335 hours per day times 233 days (from Step 3) equal 1,942 available hours to earn your goal from Step 1.

Step 5. What you are worth every single minute! The last step is to take your income goal from Step 1 (e.g., $187,500) and divide it by the available hours to get your hourly worth and then divide that hourly number by sixty to get your worth every single minute.

Example: $187,500 divided by 1,942 equal $96.55/hour divided by 60 (minutes/hour) equal $1.61 per minute!

Step 6. Take a look at where you are spending each minute of each working day. The goal of this exercise is to reinforce your incredible value each minute of each day so you focus! We recommend you write your value per minute (Example: $1.61)in four places:

1. Your cell phone/PDA. Print out a very small $1.61 label and tape it on your cell phone where you will see it when a call, text message or e-mail comes in. Do you really want to take that call right now? Do you really want to stop what you are focused on doing and decrease your efficiency?

2. Your office phone. Print out a very small $1.61 label and tape it on your office phone. Similar to your cell phone/PDA you want to be aware of the value of every minute of your time as you reach for the phone.

3. Your computer screen/planner. Print out a very small $1.61label and tape it near your computer screen. This could be your laptop, desktop or wherever you receive e-mails and manage your calendar. When you receive the e-mail do you really want to address it right now?

4. Your speedometer. Print out a very small $1.61 label and tape it near the speedometer of your vehicle. When you jump behind the wheel after agreeing to "stop by" on what you realize is a poorly qualified opportunity you will take a look at the value of your time! Perhaps it's best to make a quick phone call and ask them a few more qualifying questions. Perhaps you should reschedule when you are going to be out on another call in their area. Those high priority tasks sit dormant while you are in traffic. Manage your commitments!

Take fifteen minutes today to calculate the value of every minute of your time and put those reminders where they will make a difference. Don't exchange your valuable dollars for a dime here or there!

DAY 14
Develop Probing Questions: Get Your Prospects Talking, Then Listen

For today gather your sales and marketing materials. We are going to identify several features, advantages and benefits for your product/service and then develop questions to engage your prospects in meaningful targeted discussion. Given the fact that you have such limited time with prospects, it is essential that you ask meaningful targeted open-ended questions that will get the prospect talking. Our goal in the initial call is to understand the needs of the prospect. Open-ended questions are ideal because they cannot be answered with a "yes" or "no" answer and are designed to get the prospect talking. If you begin a question with Who, What, When, Where, Why or How, it typically becomes an open-ended question.

Take your sales literature and make a list of the top Features (F) and Advantages (A) associated with your product or service. Then, for each F/A ask the question "So what?" Because that's exactly what the prospect is asking themselves. Visualize the prospect standing in front of you asking the question, "So what? How will that benefit me?" The answer should ultimately result in a benefit your prospect would experience. Do the same for each Advantage associated with your product/service. When you're done you should have a list of benefits the prospect will experience for each Feature and Advantage.

Next, take each benefit and ask yourself the question "what situation, problem or challenge would a prospect need to have in order to desire this benefit, feature or advantage with my product?"

Take each situation, problem or challenge you wrote down and create an open-ended question that asks if they have that situation, problem or challenge.

Congratulations. You now have a series of good, probing questions to identify whether a prospect might benefit from your product or service. Remember, if your client does not think they have a need, then you are going to have to work a lot harder to convince them they need your product. Why not qualify prospects earlier in the process with these targeted meaningful questions so you don't waste your valuable time on low potential situations?

Remember, your prospects have very little time so you can't run through every single benefit of your product/service hoping they will hear something they want. By asking these meaningful targeted questions up front the prospects are talking and you are learning what your sales strategy should be for the balance of the call.

Practice the questions *out loud* until you feel comfortable asking them without having to read them.

DAY 15
Networking...Or Creating Collisions:
Start by Saying Hello

Much has been written about networking and prospecting. While the two terms are often interchanged, you should think of them as separate strategies. Networking is the process of meeting people, learning about them, helping them and *linking* them into *your* network. I often refer to networking as "creating collisions". Every moment you are awake you should be looking for ways to "collide" with someone whom you can help and/or who can help you. Everyone has a network whether or not they think of it as such. Their network might involve no more than a few close friends and their family, but it is their network. Your goal is to expand the network of people you know and provide value within that network. When you provide value, the network grows.

First Things First

Get their name while making a positive first impression! One of the early lessons I learned was to take the initiative in networking. Don't wait for someone to connect with you; go out and create the connection. The following two variations are simple but powerful ways to greet people in a networking environment:

1. Walk up to them, extend your hand and simply say, "Jim Ryerson (your name). And you are. . . ?"

2. "Good Evening/Morning/Afternoon/Hello (as you reach out and extend your hand say your name) Jim Ryerson. And you are. . . ?"

The key is to leave the pause at the end of "And you are?" Understand that 99.9 percent of the time this will put them in a place where they absolutely must say their name! Now you have their name, which is a very important first step!

Keep holding their handshake until they say their name. While this short greeting and handshake takes only three to five seconds, a lot is going on in the mind of the person you are greeting.

First, you approached them confidently, and that makes a very positive first impression. Second, you extended your hand, which is an act of "giving." You are extending yourself, and that makes a very positive first impression. Third, by saying your name first, with confidence, you create a presumption in their mind that you are "someone" and that makes a very positive first impression. Fourth, you have offered your name and now by asking them their name ("And you are. . .?"), your request is not unreasonable. Fifth, once you have their name you will start addressing them by their first name — since people like to hear their name.

Go ahead and pick one of the two variations above and say it *out loud* at least twenty times. If you are too self-conscious about having someone hear you talking to yourself then go outside, in your car, or wherever you can get away and practice this while extending your hand, as if to shake the hand of a networking prospect.

The engaging eye and smile

When you approach someone with this greeting, it's essential that you look them in the eye and smile. Over 55 percent of what they will take away from this first encounter with you will come from your body language. It's certainly not going to come from the words you say so we're going to keep the words to a minimum. As a result, I recommend making eye contact by looking at one eye, and only one eye, as you approach the person you are going to greet. And don't forget to have a pleasant, welcoming smile! Approach them with a smile, greet them, hold that hand, and look into their eye until they say their name. Once you are comfortable with this single greeting statement then stand in front of a mirror and do it again, this time walking toward the mirror and extending your hand.

Note: Don't go ahead to the next day's reading until you have mastered this simple networking greeting. Too often we practice in our mind and feel as though we have the technique mastered. You seldom get a second chance at a first impression. This greeting is often the first impression that the other person will develop when meeting you. It's essential that your voice be smooth, comfortable, and inviting. Once you've mastered this short greeting you will find it flows without thought, and your mind can focus on remembering their name and beginning the LINK process.

Do not move forward until you have mastered this greeting!

Remember to remember that name!

When I travel around the world, I ask this question to every audience: "How many of you forget a person's name right after they introduce themselves?" Believe it or not, it's typically 80 percent of the audience that raises their hands. So there's nothing wrong with you because you forget a name. You're in good company.

There's a lot of pressure on you when you first get into networking. One of the results of that pressure is you tend to try too hard to remember too much. I recommend that you focus on and remember the first name. Typically, last names are more complex and your brain is trying so hard to figure out how to remember the last name, we forget the first. Then the alarm sounds in our brain because we can't remember the first name. You hear your conscience saying, "What's the first name? I can't believe you forgot the first name. What a loser." This does not do much for your self-confidence, and it often changes your demeanor during this critical first impression.

As they say their first and last name, just recall the first name, and say it to yourself while they are in the process of saying their last name. Your brain works five to seven times faster than your mouth. You can repeat their first name a few times in your mind during the same period of time they are saying their last name out loud. Remember, if after talking to this prospect you feel like you can bring value to them, you will most likely get their card and you will have their last name anyway.

Next, immediately say their name out loud with a simple statement and ask an open-ended question that requires them to talk. Follow this process again from start to finish:

> You (as you walk toward them with your hand extended toward their right hand): Jim Ryerson. And you are. . . ?

> Prospect: Sally Delaney. (You say to yourself, Sally, Sally.)

> You: Hi, Sally, nice to meet you. So, Sally, what brings you here?

By saying their first name immediately, you will cement it in your mind for the duration of this initial conversation. I recommend using their first name occasionally, since people love to hear their name. Incidentally, they've probably already forgotten yours, so give them your card before you end your conversation.

Why the open-ended question? Rather than talk about the weather, the food, the traffic, or another inconsequential topic, you actually begin to qualify. The best networkers are always qualifying as early as possible. Why waste your valuable selling time on prospects to whom you can bring no value?

You can select from several alternative open-ended questions based on the venue:

- If this is an association meeting, then your question may be "Sally, nice to meet you. What brings you here?" (As noted above.)

- If this is a soccer game with your kids your question may be "Sally, nice to meet you. Who are you here to watch?"

Ultimately, you want to get to the short question "What do you do?" You have to decide when it's appropriate. Keep in mind, though, that not asking the question puts you behind so get over your concern about being too forward and ask the question!

Practice this greeting out loud until you have it down. Begin using it immediately!

DAY 16
Make Your LINK: Get to Know Your Prospects Starting with Their Line of Work

To help you put a structure or process in place for networking, I want you to think about the word LINK. I use LINK because that's what you're really doing when you go out and network. You link yourself with the person you meet, and you link the person you meet with others in your network. And while it might not be evident at that time, you may link the person you meet with your strategy for a potential sale.

Each letter in the word LINK stands for something. It's an acronym for the four types of information needed to help someone with your network. Each of the next four days we will deal with one of the letters.

L is for Line

First, find out what Line they are in. You may think this is extremely easy because it's on their business card. However, you want to dig deeper into what they do versus just their title.

Ask some questions about what they do. The following are some sample questions:

- "What type of selling are you involved with?"

- "What areas do you focus on as president?"

- "What does your typical week consist of?"

- "What areas are you responsible for?"

Get them talking. People love to talk about themselves. When you develop your qualification questions later in the book you may have several questions to help qualify them as prospective clients. However, don't make the mistake of dismissing people in a networking venue just because they are not a good prospect. One of the goals of networking is to grow your network, and everyone is a potential for your network.

Let's set the stage so you can place yourself in a common situation as you learn about the LINK strategy. You're at a networking venue put on by a local organization. You know a few people there but there are many people you've never met. Most salespeople head into these engagements with the intent of hanging out with people they know, talking about life, and leaving once they've had their fill of food. A sales professional will acknowledge the people they know, but since these folks are already part of their network there's very little gain – in a networking sense – from spending the evening with them. The sales professional looks for an opportunity to "collide" with someone they haven't met.

Because you have mastered your greeting from Day 15 you will take the initiative to greet someone. After they say their name, greet them with their first name: "Nice to meet you, Kate." Ask them what brought them there, or make another observation from their nametag. The key is to eventually get to, "So, Kate, what do you do?"

Continue to ask questions about what they do since people love to talk about themselves. The person will usually ask "What about you," or "What do you do?" Be careful not to use a slick, polished, professional overview. While this "sound bite" may sound good on a voice mail, it rarely puts the prospect at ease or engages them in a conversation. These "commercials" are fantastic when prospecting on the phone or in person on a sales call, but they have no place in the networking environment. Instead, share what you do quickly and succinctly and then look for an opening to move the conversation back to them and their situation. Seldom, if ever, does a sale occur in a networking situation. As a result you want to avoid pushing your product or service and focus on the prospect.

For today, create a short, succinct statement about what you do so you are prepared when they ask!

DAY 17
LINK to Interests: Find Out What They Do for Fun

Today we'll work on the next step in the LINK process. Once you have some information about what line they are in you want to know what Interests they have. This may take a few questions like, "Where are you from?" "Have you always lived in this location?" "Are you originally from this area?" Based on the networking venue, you may already have a start on this (medical gathering, religious organization, etc.). One of my favorite questions to get this type of information is, "What do you do for fun?" People love to talk about themselves, and they really like to talk about their passions. So why not ask them about their Interests?

When you think about the LINK process, I want you to visualize a manual merry-go-round at a playground. If you have a few children on the merry-go-round it takes a fair amount of effort and energy to get it moving. You grab hold of the merry-go-round and start to push it. You dig your feet into the dirt as you run faster and faster and push the merry-go-round harder and harder. Then, once you get it up to speed you stand off to the side and simply give it a good push every so often to keep it going.

This is how the LINK process of questioning works:

- First, we have to intentionally approach new people and introduce ourselves.

- Then we have to ask intentional, focused questions to get them talking.

- But once we get them talking it takes less effort to keep the conversation going and learn about them!

Don't be in a hurry to move beyond the Interests conversation. This is where you develop a rapport with the person. The odd thing is they are typically doing most of the talking. Common areas that come up during the Interests conversation include their children, their business, sports, coaching, family, art, travel, music, and the list goes on. The key is to get them talking about themselves and make a mental note of these Interests for later.

Don't push too hard

All of this is part of the selling process, but it can't be too obvious. One of the major errors salespeople make in networking environments is they push too hard and too fast regarding business opportunities.

Think about it this way. If you're a salesperson, should you really expect to get a sale the first time you meet someone? The answer is typically, "Absolutely not. My selling process takes a few weeks, months, years, etc." Since people buy for personal and emotional reasons, why would we take a chance turning them off by pushing too hard the first time we meet?

The best result is that the prospect is comfortable with you, likes you, and enjoys talking with you. Most often, that means it should not feel like a sales call, where they feel like they are being "sold." So if you don't move beyond the Interests step during your initial contact, that's fine! You're not going to make the sale during the first networking encounter, so you need to make that engagement as positive and "non-selling" as you can. That's why it's so important to qualify the person during that initial contact. If you find they are truly a prospect, you will follow up with them later.

Stick with the Interest step and keep them talking about what they love to do, listen for a connection, and get their business card or contact information.

DAY 18
LINK to Needs: Bring Value to the People You Meet

The next step in the LINK networking process is to find out what Needs people have. Their Needs are important because they open the door for you to bring value. That's what networking is about: bringing value to the people you meet. However, you cannot ask, "So, what are some of your Needs?" That would not create the type of conversational comfort you are trying to develop. Therefore, Needs is often the most difficult of the four LINK steps to master.

Do not be surprised if you don't hear any Needs the first few times you use this process. Catching Needs statements is a learned skill, and your ability to listen and hear their Needs will improve over time.

Needs statements often occur around their discussion of the Line they are in or their Interests. Listen carefully for words that suggest some of the following needs:

- Dissatisfaction in their current Line: "I've been there way too long." "We're really struggling right now." "We've just implemented a new program and it's really a mess." "Things are going well but we need to get more business for the future." "I'm trying to figure out what to do next."

- Dissatisfaction around their Interests: "I'm working/traveling so much I rarely get a chance to play." "My weekends are so SECTION 3: Networking busy I rarely have a minute to myself." "I hurt my knee and I'm not able to play basketball." "I wish I could improve my golf game." "I wish I had more time to read."

- Desire to improve something with their Line: "Things are going well right now but we need to figure out how to..." "I'd like to be doing (a better position/role) with a company in the next few years." "I need to figure out how to master (a particular issue)."

- Desire to improve something with their Interests: "My goal is to get more time at the practice range this year." "I really want to learn how to (activity) this year." "I've always wanted to go to (location)."

Since most of the Needs around a Line pertain to either dissatisfaction with their Line or a desire to improve something with their Line, here are several questions that might keep the conversation moving:

- "What is it like working there?"

- "How do you like the role you're in?"

- "What is the next step for someone in your position?"

Since most of the Needs pertain to a challenge or obstacle that's getting in the way of their Interest, here are several questions you could ask:

- "How often do you get a chance to...?"

- "How often do you want to get out and...?"

- "When do you find the time to...?"

Keep a mental note of what you hear them say about their Needs. It's important to recognize that many of their Needs may have nothing to do with business. You can start relationships with many prospects by providing value not related to their business, for example, an article or note about a recreational, personal, family, or sport need that they have. By paying attention to these Needs and providing value, you begin to develop a personal and emotional bond.

It takes a long time to develop a network. This investment in bringing "non-business" value to others is a long-term investment. It will pay off, but it takes time.

DAY 19
Sales Octane Mantra #5—Your Network Is Your Net Worth

In 1967, psychologist Stanley Milgram conducted an interesting experiment to try and determine whether we are all connected in some grand network. Milgram got the names of 160 people in Omaha, Nebraska and mailed each of them a packet that included the name and address of a stockbroker who worked in Boston and lived in Sharon, Massachusetts. Each person was instructed to write their name on a slip of paper in the packet and send the packet on to a friend or acquaintance they knew who might get the packet closer to the stockbroker in Massachusetts (without sending it to the stockbroker directly). If you had a friend who lived on the east coast, for instance, you might send the packet to them because it's closer to Boston, Massachusetts. That person would then put their name on the packet and send it to someone they knew that might get it to the stockbroker. When the packet finally arrived at the stockbroker they identified how many steps it took to get the package from Omaha to this specific person in Boston.

How many people, on average, would you think the packet would go through to get from Omaha, Nebraska to a specific person in Sharon, Mass? The answer to that question led to the popular phrase and John Guare's 1990 play of the same name, Six Degrees of Separation. Milgram found that, on average, you are approximately six people from the person you need to get to.

Here's the catch, this was back in 1967 before the advent of the Internet, cell phones, Instant Messaging, Text Messaging, Google, Social Networking (Instagram, Facebook, etc.), contact management programs, and before people routinely migrated away from their place of birth. Today it is much easier to connect than ever before.

Each additional contact your meet exponentially increases your network since you have the opportunity to connect into their network! Recent online share-ware products such as LinkedIn and FaceBook, are two examples of a formalized approach to this concept. Sales professionals who understand the power of networking will leverage every one of these tools.

Identify the tools mentioned in today's information and join the solution that best fits your needs. Finally, if you don't have a contact management system you must invest in one as soon as possible. Whether you use a computer based software or an online approach you must begin to manage your contact list as you would your checkbook! Enter information found during Day 17 into your contact database. This way, you will quickly and efficiently LINK and retrieve important contacts. Once you join these programs, your ongoing investment of time is minimal! Expand your network and expand your net worth. It works!

DAY 20
Sales Octane Mantra #6—Creating Real Value Is Not Just About the Product or Service You Sell!

Creating value is a buzzword that typically focuses on the benefits your customers experience when they use your product or service. When we say Creating Value we go beyond the benefits a customer experiences with the use of your product and service. Creating Real Value can be the positive effect you have on others. It can be your smile, the thank you note you send. It's the way you greet people, the way you reinforce them honestly and sincerely. And it can be the extra mile you go for others. Creating Real Value is anything you do for another person that helps them! Work hard, work with integrity and create real value and your success is assured.

DAY 21
LINK to Know: Learn About What and Whom They Know

Since networking is about bringing value to others, then understanding what a new contact is knowledgeable about is essential. That understanding enables you to connect them to someone else in your network that Needs what/whom they Know.

Most contacts are more than happy to share what they Know and whom they Know if given the chance. But we are usually so focused on telling everyone what we do that we never learn anything about the person we are talking with. Worse, the person we are talking with walks away with a feeling that the world revolves around us and our experiences and that we don't really care about them.

Think about a recent social or business event where you met someone new, and all they did was speak about themselves. How did you feel about that engagement? Chances are you wanted to interject and say something about your experiences with the topic. Chances are you thought to yourself, "My gosh, does this person ever come up for air?" Maybe you thought, "This person seems quite self-centered." In most cases, you did not walk away with a warm and fuzzy feeling that this is someone you want to head out for lunch with the following day! Why? Because the conversation was totally about them and you wanted some airtime.

Now, how do you think they felt about that conversation? They probably went home and mentioned how they had a "wonderful conversation" with you! They probably really enjoyed it. Chances are, if you called them the following day and said you enjoyed the "conversation" and wanted to have lunch with them to chat some more, they would agree because they felt like it was a great "conversation."

The LINK process helps you get the focus off you and get the focus on the prospect. It helps create a positive emotion about you so you can move forward with the prospect. In this situation everyone wins. They'll walk away feeling like they had a great conversation. You walk away knowing about the Line they are in, their Interests, what they Need, what they Know and whom they Know. You'll walk away with information that can help you bring value to the prospect and possibly develop a business relationship if you identified an opportunity during the conversation.

In order to get them to share their area of Knowledge, make an occasional observation when you hear them get engaged in a topic. For instance, if they are speaking about their Line and they become quite animated, you could make the observation, "It seems like you have a real passion about (their Line). Is this something you've always been interested in?" This gets the conversation going deeper around their Knowledge and may even open up a connection to whom they Know. Probe!

Another good question is, "Where did you go to school?" Depending on the level of education they have achieved, you will be able to pick up on their comfort level with this topic. However, the contact is usually quick to offer the college or university they attended. Then ask a follow-up question: "What was your major?" You will learn whether their area of Interest started during their education and has continued on in their profession, or they will talk about how they chose a different path once they were out of school. In either case, you should pick up some signals on where to go with the questioning. If they become animated and engaged with a path of discussion then continue to move down that path. If you sense them disconnecting (eyes beginning to look at everyone around the room, short answers, etc.), then move in another direction.

Often their Knowledge results from their Interest. When they become very engaged and animated about the discussion of their Interest, simply make the observation: "It sounds like you Know a lot about..." Or "How did you get so involved with...?"

The Know step is the least understood and the most frequently abused of all the steps in the LINK process. Many clients try to force their way into getting names from contacts in an effort to drop those same names with others in a lame attempt at networking.

Who someone knows is a very personal piece of information that must be treated with extreme caution. At the same time, whom they Know is often the most valuable LINK you will uncover. Most often a person will share the name of someone they Know in the course of a networking conversation. It may be the name of someone they work with, the name of a major customer, a friend or business acquaintance.

If a contact mentions the name of a company that you have targeted in your Wish 100 from Day 9, it is important to find out whom they Know at that company. The question must be positioned in an off-handed way, possibly later in the conversation, "I've been focusing on them for several months. Whom do you know there?" However, they may be reluctant to toss out a name. If you feel them shutting down after the question, simply make a honest positive observation about the target company and move on to another topic. You can raise the question another day.

If the contact mentions a name that interests you, be cautious about showing visual signs of heightened awareness. Remember, LINKing is about the prospect and not about you! Keep the conversation going without appearing self-serving. Ask, "Oh, Sally Smith. How long have you known Sally?" The length of time a contact has known a key target is a great indication of the type of true relationship they have.

Find out what they know and who they know and you're on your way!

DAY 22
Accumulate LINK Information:
Make a Note of It

At each point in the LINK process I made the comment, "Make a mental note." That's because in a networking environment, it is often unacceptable to make written notes whenever you pick up information that may help you LINK with the contact. However, there is often critical information that you must capture. I recommend using the contact's business card for that purpose.

When the timing is right you should make a reinforcing statement such as "It sounds like you have a great company/product" or "I've really enjoyed our conversation" — whatever is an honest and sincere statement. Then, take one of your business cards and offer it to them with the statement/request, "Here's my business card, do you have a card?" The fact that you gave them your card first creates an obligation in them to give you their card. If they don't have a card with them then it's fine for you to say "No problem, I have another card, just write down your name and contact information." Either way you walk away with their contact information on a card.

Once you have a quiet moment write down the LINK information you've gathered on the back of the business card. Use one corner for Line information, another corner for Interest, another corner for Needs, and the final corner for what they Know and whom they Know. Also write the date and where you met (the venue, association meeting, kids' softball game, specific meeting, etc.) in the center of the back of all the cards you accumulate.

Now you have all the pertinent information regarding the conversation and it is tied to the name of the client. This process also makes it easier for an associate to key the information into your contact database. You'll never need to ask yourself, "Whom did I meet last week that mentioned that company?" Or "Here's their card. But where/when did I meet them?" As you improve your LINKing skills, you will find it difficult to keep up with all the business cards you accumulate.

Another reason to write on the back of a business card versus the front is that it may cause a problem with a card-scanning device or service.

DAY 23
Overt and Covert LINKing of Contacts: Using Your Network to Help Others

It's inevitable. After you begin the LINK networking process, a contact will mention a Need and you will Know someone in your network that has information about that area of Need. For instance, you meet someone who shares with you that their business is growing, and they are looking at branching out into another geographic market — let's say another state. You remember that you have someone in your network who already has a business in that same state. You may chose to mention this immediately in a very overt fashion and follow up with a communication providing all the contact information.

This works. But it's so overt it may appear to be self-serving. We never want contacts to feel like we are asking a hundred questions in hopes that we can respond with something. Remember this important point: in any type of a purchase that involves a salesperson, the buyer typically buys based on a personal and emotional connection. They often use facts and figures to justify to others why they made the purchase but it starts with a strong personal and emotional connection. We like to say that people buy from people! As a result, at this early stage of our relationship we want to stay focused on getting them comfortable with us. So let's try LINKing more covertly with contacts.

Here's the same situation, using a less direct approach. You meet someone and they share with you that their business is growing and they are looking at branching out into another state. You remember that you have someone in your network who already has a business in that same state. In this scenario, you keep learning about them and don't immediately LINK them to your contact. Instead, you stay in form and continue to ask questions and learn more about them. Probe more about their Line, Interest, and Knowledge. Don't forget, this may be your one and only time to gather LINK information in hopes of helping them in the future. After you've left the conversation, make a note on the back of the contact's business card about their Need to expand into the new state. Also, jot a reminder to LINK them to your other contact in that state.

After your networking event, you get back to your office and put together a quick e-mail to both the contact who is planning to expand into the new state and to the contact who is already running a company in that state. Put both e-mail addresses in the "Send To" line so there's no differentiation. Then say something like this in the body of the e-mail:

Kate, (new contact) meet Bob (in your existing network). Bob runs a successful business in California, and after learning about your interest in California last evening, I thought Bob might be able to shed some light on the issue. That's it, have a great day. Jim

Do not follow up with Kate to see if she called Bob, or even with Bob to see if Kate called him. If you make follow-up calls, it will appear that you are LINKing Kate and Bob simply because you're hoping Kate will be grateful to you. It seldom works and you'll get a reputation as someone who uses contacts for personal gain. Remember that the goal is to foster an environment that results in collisions, but you don't want to be seen as a traffic cop directing cars into each other. LINK them up and move on!

There's another reason to use the less direct route. The information you learned might be a perfect reason to reconnect with the contact for a later call or meeting. Typically you will have traded business cards so you have a way to connect with them in the future.

The goal of networking is to create collisions. You want to create an environment where you are "running into" or colliding with opportunities. One way to do this is to get so much activity going on around you that your name is being mentioned often *in the context of helping others using your network!*

As you continue to use the process you will improve your ability to file away key names and issues that surface as the contact is talking. In the beginning, simply head off to another room for a minute after your conversation and jot down your notes in the format we mentioned. Over time you'll be able to keep information in your head from two to three people and then transfer it to the business cards later, out of the flow of the networking event.

The great thing about LINK is that it positions your future conversations. You have key information to make meaningful conversation, and you are always looking for other Needs that your contact has, along with their Knowledge and who they Know. The Needs and Know/Knowledge are the two areas that will be the most dynamic over time and are often the source of the greatest connections.

DAY 24
Beyond LINK: Baseline Contact Information

Aside from LINK information, over time you will want to gather and store several other pieces of information that are helpful as you build your business.

Correct pronunciation of the contact's name

Spell it out phonetically so you are confident you will say their name properly. As simple as it sounds, many an opportunity to LINK has been lost by the salesperson constantly mispronouncing the contact's name. So write down the way the name is pronounced and don't leave it to chance!

E-mail/Phone/Website/Mobile

This is self-evident.

Birthday

Believe it or not, this is a great source of connection. Figure out when and where they were born. In many cases you'll be able to LINK others in your network that were born or raised in the same area. Many sales professionals also send a birthday card or note to the key contacts in their database. Put a reminder in your computer a week or so before the date you can send a note and leave another positive impression. Don't use an insincere, preprinted address label for a birthday card.

College/University/Education

Another point of conversation during the LINK process might be where the contact attended school. This allows you to LINK others in your network that may have attended the same institution. Keep in mind that in some states, this may also mean their high school! I remember how shocked I was several years ago when I asked, "Where did you go to school?" and the response centered on their high school experience. I disguised my surprise and found out later that in that area, the high school was the key.

Current and past co-workers

If the contact works with someone with whom you have had a relationship, then you can connect with that person to gather other relevant information for your strategy. It may take some time to develop a rapport before this kind of information is discussed.

DAY 25
Give to Receive: Follow "The Golden Rule"

When you give, you receive. It's a fact of life. However, that's *not* why we give! We give because it fits with the Golden Rule: Do unto others as you would have them do unto you.

Think of all the benefits you would receive if everyone you met brought you some value from the people in their network. Think of all the benefits you would receive if everyone you met took the time to truly understand your business and the Needs you have for additional prospects — and then gave you a list of names from their network that could use your product/service! It would be unbelievable. And you are the person who is going to begin that process.

When you use your network to help others, you will eventually see a response from people connecting you back to others in their network. That's the concept behind networking. The next time you *give*, don't expect anything in return, but be prepared because it will happen.

DAY 26
Sales Octane Mantra #7—There Is No Such Thing as a Free Lunch: Putting Obligation and Reciprocity to Work

If you've ever been on the receiving end of a "free lunch" you've probably been influenced by the principles of obligation and reciprocity. It may have been a time where someone took you out for lunch and mentioned at the end of the meal that they needed help that weekend taking in their boat dock. Like it or not, the meal created a sense of obligation to your friend. Then, when they asked if you would help you felt the need to reciprocate. These two principles — obligation and reciprocity — worked together to create a triggered response and off you went to pull out their boat dock. While you may have helped them regardless of the lunch, the principle of obligation and reciprocity definitely improved the odds that you would say "YES."

The principle is simple. By giving someone something, anything, you obligate them. The round of golf, tickets to the theatre, dinner, thank you/holiday notes and even a simple "thank you" can be used to create obligation on behalf of the recipient. Then, when you ask them for something, even something of greater value, the sense of obligation causes them to reciprocate. This triggered response can be put to work with your prospects and customers. We will use this principle throughout this book. Here are several examples for each step of the Sales Continuum where obligation and reciprocity apply.

Networking - You can use the principle of obligation and reciprocity when you meet someone for the first time. For example, using the LINK process you identify their passion for golf so you send them an article on improving their golf game and even throw in some golf accessories. When you follow up in a few weeks to request an appointment you have improved your odds of their agreement! Obligation leads to reciprocity.

Prospecting – When you finally get through to a prospect and they request that you send them specific information you can use the principle of obligation and reciprocity. When you follow through and send them the information they requested you remind them in the cover note that you are sending this as requested and then ask them for an appointment to discuss the information. Obligation leads to reciprocity.

Qualifying – Use the principle of obligation and reciprocity when you're making calls to a list of attendees from an association trade show where you had a booth. When you mention the fact that you had a booth at their association's trade show and it was great to support their association you remind them of the fact that you contributed to their association. This improves your odds of a warmer reception so they will answer your qualifying questions and agree to the next step. Obligation leads to reciprocity.

Appointment – When you are face to face or phone to phone with the prospect you can use the principles of obligation and reciprocity. As you uncover their problems ask them "If I were able to solve that problem, and I'm not saying I can right now, but if I could, is that what you're looking for?/Would you be willing to move forward with our product/service?" Their positive response obligates them to reciprocate. Then, if you're able to resolve their problem they are more inclined to reciprocate than if you had simply given them a solution without their obligation.

Trial Closing – The principles of obligation and reciprocity work particularly well with detail oriented individuals (Driven/Dominant and Compliant/Analytical Behavioral Styles from Day 2) when you begin trial closing. By consistently asking "Is this helpful?", "Is this what you wanted?" and "Is this what you were looking for?" the prospect will obligate themselves when they answer in the affirmative. You've given them what they wanted and this triggers their obligation. Ultimately they are more inclined to reciprocate in the future when you ask for the next step.

Closing – After you've closed a sale you can use the principles of obligation and reciprocity to ensure the customer follows through despite buyer's remorse or conflicting direction from other team members. Once they say "yes," take a few moments to share with them the details of what you will be doing next now that they have decided to move forward. This creates a sense of obligation to you and they will reciprocate by making sure they "sell" to others who might want to second guess their decision.

Referral – Use the principles of obligation and reciprocity when asking for referrals. By covering all the things you have done for the customer and reinforcing the value you have brought them they become obligated. When you ask for referrals, that obligation causes them to reciprocate and provide you with more referrals than you otherwise might have received.

There are two excellent books on this topic that are worth the investment of time: *Influence, The Psychology of Persuasion* by Robert B. Cialdini, PhD, and *The Power Of Persuasion, How We're Bought And Sold* by Robert Levine. Look for ways to use obligation in your sales process and you will find that prospects and customers are more inclined to reciprocate when you ask for their help!

DAY 27
Sales Octane Mantra #8—Whatever You Reinforce You Get More Of

Beginning with the research of Skinner and Pavlov (does "ring the bell and the dog drools" sound familiar?) research confirms that when someone is reinforced for doing something they will be more likely to continue doing that "something." For instance, if my daughter is studying at the dining room table and I come by and reinforce her, she is more inclined to study more often. If I reinforce my daughter with a reward, say a trip to the ice cream store, when she has a great report card I am improving the probability that she will do more of whatever she did to secure the grades. This continues in the workforce. If your sales manager reinforces you by recognizing your recent order they are improving the probability you will do more of whatever you did to get that order. The reason is simple. The recipient of the reinforcement—my daughter or you—genuinely likes the reinforcement. They like the recognition, they like the rewards and they like the reinforcement. While this makes sense when you read the examples above, it's even more important as an application for salespeople with prospects or customers.

Whenever you reinforce a prospect or customer, honestly and sincerely, they like you more. I'm not talking about insincerely blowing smoke. I'm talking about honestly and sincerely reinforcing your prospects and customers. Look for positive results their company or their department has achieved. Look for positive accomplishments they have achieved both personally and professionally. Look for positive accomplishments of their family members, alma mater, associations they belong to, their city, etc. One of my favorite reinforcements is when I learn that a prospect/customer's favorite sports team has accomplished something positive. I send them an e-mail, text message or voice mail referencing the great game. The responses I get back are always positive! Look for anything you can reinforce, honestly and sincerely, and watch over time what happens. You will become a positive reinforcing light in an otherwise negative, aversive and dark world. You will separate yourself from your competition. You will brand yourself as a positive reinforcing person and people like people that are positive and reinforcing.

For today, take your top ten prospects and/or customers and identify one single reinforcement you can make, honestly and sincerely. Send them an e-mail, note or tie it in with a business call. Watch how they respond! Whatever you reinforce you get more of!

Note: this has great application with everyone: friends, family members, co-workers, and the person you meet on the street.

DAY 28
More Eyes and Ears Equal More Opportunities

As you begin to meet people through your networking efforts you will uncover a number of opportunities. At the same time, there is another excellent source of leads and opportunities and we call this process the Wheel of the Fortunate. Most of the opportunities you identify are the direct result of your efforts, your ears hearing of an opportunity, your eyes seeing an opportunity, your feet walking by/up to an opportunity and your hands working the phone, Internet, newspaper and computer in an effort to identify an opportunity.

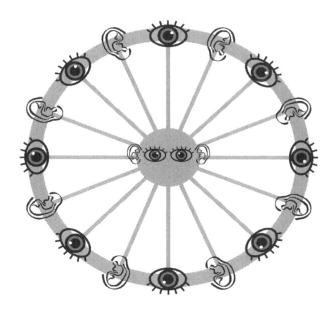

Similar to any wheel, the larger the diameter the more distance can be traveled with less revolutions and effort. It may take more effort to get a larger diameter wheel rolling but it covers a lot more ground with less effort! This is the concept that drives the Wheel of the Fortunate.

The concept is simple. There are often many other products and/or services that your prospects acquire at approximately the same time they evaluate buying your product or service. At the same time, there are salespeople who sell those other products/services that do not compete with you. If you can create a relationship with even a few of the top sales professionals at these companies you will begin to develop a solid source of leads and referrals.

At the end of this next effort you will have many eyes, ears, feet, and hands working on your behalf and it will not cost anything! This is not to be confused with the "paid" networking groups. While these groups can be beneficial, you will not typically find the top sales professionals in these groups since they have a solid base of business and a lead network of their own. It's okay to belong to paid networking groups but not at the expense of The Wheel of the Fortunate!

First, list your first product or service you sell on a piece of paper. Next, answer the question, "What conditions exist when someone buys this product or service?" Write the list of these conditions below the product or service. For example, if you sell office furniture then some of the conditions are as follows: the prospect is moving, the prospects lease is up, the prospect has a growing business and is hiring people or the prospect has acquired a company and is planning to absorb additional employees. If you sell life insurance then some of the conditions are as follows: the prospect has a new position and the increased income demands increased life insurance, the prospect gets married, the prospect has children, and so on.

One exercise you can do to determine these conditions is to reverse engineer several recent sales opportunities. Why did they begin looking for your product or service? This will typically lead you to a set of conditions that drives interest in your product or service. Keep in mind that if you sell numerous products/services, there may be different conditions for each product or service.

The more overlap, the less choices you'll need to make. However, the more choices you have, the more opportunities you have to develop this important lead network. Take time today to create a list of conditions that occur for each product or service category you sell. Share the list with your peers, superiors, and anyone who might be able to help you identify additional conditions.

DAY 29
Customers Buy Other Products And Services at the Same Time They Need Your Product or Service...Right?

Take each condition you identified yesterday and list every other product or service someone might purchase in addition to your product/service. For example, let's take the first condition: the prospect is moving. List the other non-competing products or services that the prospect may also acquire or evaluate *at the same time*. For instance, when someone moves they typically hire a mover, work with a commercial real estate broker, evaluate new phone systems, cabling, computers, copiers, carpeting, lighting, plants, coffee machines, water dispensers, security systems, etc. Go through each condition and come up with as many other non-competing products or services as you can think of. Go for the high numbers; ten to fifteen different non-competing products and services would be fantastic. Share your list of products and services with other peers and your superiors to identify additional products/services.

Note: it's essential to get as many products/services identified as you can. Keep a running list as you may wish to add others to your networking group as you move forward.

DAY 30
The Best Companies Have The Best Leads

Take each product or service from your list developed on Day 29 and identify the *best* provider(s) for that product/service in your area. In many cases the best provider will change from territory to territory. It's essential that you identify the *best* provider for the following reasons:

First, as discussed earlier, people buy from people for personal and emotional reasons and then justify their decision with facts and figures. They buy from people they like. If you're going to be known as the *best* provider of your product/service in the market then it's essential that you pair yourself with the *best* provider of other products and services in your market. In effect, the lead partners you develop from the Wheel of the Fortunate process will provide a sort of "reference" for you to many prospects. As you nurture these relationships you will begin to see that solid personal and emotional ties that your lead partners have with their customers and clients will transfer over to you. While it is not the same as having that relationship yourself, the probability of securing an appointment is substantially improved by the fact that your lead partner has referred you. Their credibility with their client will, to a certain extent, become your credibility with the prospect (for your goods and/or services).

Second, the *best* companies have more customers, more market knowledge and more lead sources. The best companies often have internal resources dedicated to identifying leads. Pair yourself with the *best!*

Here are several ideas how to identify that list.

Share your list with an existing large client and ask them who they use for each product and service. If the client is large then they are probably using a good vendor. Ask your client why they chose the vendor and ask them if they feel the vendor is still a good provider! Ask your client who else they evaluated and what they thought of each of these other providers. Share with the client that you are working on a project to define the best providers of goods and services in your market and you'd like their input.

Give them a category and ask, "How about (product/service category)? Who have you heard is the best provider in our market?" Don't be too quick to talk! For each category they provide a company name, ask "Why?" or "What about them makes you think they are a great vendor?" Ask this line of questioning for each product/ service category you've identified on Day 29 so you get as many companies' and salespeople's names as possible. You should also ask them who else in their organization may be able to help you with the categories they were unable to address as they may have different buyers who handle those other categories. Ask your client if the salesperson is one of the reasons they enjoy working with the company. If so, ask for the salesperson's name.

Take a walk to the phone book. Whoever has the largest advertisement is often one of the larger providers. Go to their website and you'll get a good indication of their size and ability.

Work your network of contacts. Send everyone in your e-mail listing and tell them you are working on a project to define the best providers of a particular good or service in your market and you'd like their input. Ask friends, family, and other business associates. The key is having the list of categories and continually adding new categories. You should never stop this process as you're only one phone call away from losing your lead partner to a move or promotion.

If you are a leader or sales manager you should keep this information as it may be a great starting point for recruiting sales talent in the future. Ask your peers and others around your company for their input.

DAY 31
The Best Salespeople Have the Best Leads

Once you have a list of the *best* providers of non-competing products and services that are purchased at about the same time your product/service is purchased you want to identify the top salespeople at these "Best in class" providers.

Similar to the *best* providers, the top salespeople have the most clients, the most leads, offer the best reference and often have the best reputation in the marketplace. If you are going to be the best in class you want to pair yourself with the best in class. This list of top salespeople may come from your conversations with your clients from Day 30.

Another option is to call into the company and introduce yourself as a salesperson who is in a non-competing business. Tell them you want to hook up with a salesperson at their company to share some leads that should be beneficial to them. Whatever name you get ask the question, "Is (person's name) one of your top salespeople?" Keep pushing until you identify the best salesperson since whatever you pair yourself with you become. Similar to the last three days, share your list with other peers and get as many top sales performers identified as you can. Develop your list of top salespeople at the non-competing companies and you're ready to go!

DAY 32
Call Your Future Lead Source!

Now that you have a list of top sales performers from Day 31 you want to make the call to them and begin the process of developing your Wheel of the Fortunate lead group!

Note: You should only focus on one sales professional for each product/service category. In some cases there will not be a fit or the individual will not be interested in networking with you to share leads/referrals. In that case you will go to another sales professional and keep trying until you find a fit.

If you received their name from one of your clients or any positive reference as to their sales ability (from a peer, business associate, etc.) you want to include that bit of information *right up front* in your call or voicemail. For instance, if you are doing business with XYZ Company and your contact mentioned the name to you and said they were a great salesperson to deal with, you want to begin your voicemail/call with "Sally Smith from XYZ Company and I were talking recently and she mentioned that you were one of the best (product/service) salespeople she works with..." This will add credibility to your voicemail and virtually guarantees a return call. It shows you've done your homework and confirms that you too are a sales professional.

Pick up the phone and contact what you believe to be the best sales professional for each of the different categories. Listed below is a script you can modify when you make the call. Make sure you practice this call several times so you're comfortable and it appears you've done this before.

Script: Example – "Good Morning Sherry, my name is Jim Ryerson and I'm with ABC Company. (If you received their name from one of your clients then start with this; "Good Morning Sherry, I was talking with Bob from XYZ company and he said you do a great job for them. My name is Jim Ryerson and I'm with ABC Company.) I was wondering if we could get together over lunch since we call on many of the same clients and we don't compete with each other. I think I can provide some insight into a number of potential prospects and maybe even make you aware of several projects you might not be aware of..."

Note: Be prepared with follow-up answers because when they call you back they will likely respond with questions like "What do you do?" or "I don't understand?" or "I'm not interested" or "How did you get my name?" Treat this just like a potential sale. Be prepared for objections. You want to mention that after you get together, they can decide if there is a fit and if not you're fine with that. Frankly, they should be flattered because you are confirming them as a top sales professional in their area. Stay after them with consistent, non-desperate, voice mails until you get them live. *Do not give up.* These connections are far too important not to follow through.

DAY 33
Sales Octane Mantra #9—You Are What You "Pair" Yourself With

We've all heard the statement "you are what you eat." The Mantra "You Are What You 'Pair' Yourself With" is a variation on that theme. "Pairing" is a psychological term used to define when we tie ourselves together with something or someone, in essence pairing ourselves with another thing. Whatever you "pair" yourself with, you "become" to your audience. When you pair yourself with a negative person or a negative statement you become negative to your audience. The word audience is meant to include anyone you are in front of or communicate with (face to face, voice mail, e-mail, written correspondence, etc.).

First, let's look at this from a non-selling situation to reinforce the concept. Let's say you are in the office and someone is standing by the coffee machine, complaining about some problems they had over the weekend. Since they are pairing themselves with a negative, the person becomes more negative to you. Conversely, let's say you came in the following day and when you went to get your coffee there was another person and they were talking about how great the weather was this weekend. Since they are pairing themselves with a positive they become more positive to you. On a very basic level this makes sense but we don't give a thought to the implications for sales!

Think about the things you speak about while you are around your customers in a selling situation. What are you pairing yourself with in those situations? Do you complain in front of your customers and talk about all the things that are wrong or do you talk about positive things? How do you talk about your team members? Do you pair yourself with positives or negatives? For today and the rest of your life "pair" yourself with the positive and watch how your customers are more receptive and positive towards you!

Note: Oftentimes this issue of positive versus negative is a result of whether a person views themselves as optimistic (positive), or pessimistic (negative). The good news is you can change and become more optimistic. In his book *Learned Optimism,* Martin E. P. Seligman Ph.D. shares the steps for how to learn to be optimistic. If you consider yourself a pessimist I strongly encourage you to read and follow the principles outlined in his book.

DAY 34
Sales Octane Mantra #10—It's What You Know, Who You Know and Who Knows You!

When I grew up I did not have position. It always bothered me when people would say, "It's not what you know it's who you know." Basically, I did not know anyone! I decided to prove the world wrong and show them that knowing a lot ("what you know") would, in fact, catapult me to success. I spent several years becoming the knowledge leader with the product and services offered by the company whose product I represented. Frankly, I became the Answer Man! Everyone would come to me for answers about product application, where to find information, etc. And while that did increase my value and wealth, it paled in comparison to those around me who had worked diligently to expand their network. What you know is essential as it increases your value, but it needs to be combined with a diligent effort to expand your network and contacts. The combination of having knowledge about your product/service and expanding your network and connections will lead to the most important step for ongoing sales success – Who knows you. You want people to think of you because of your knowledge and because you are connected via the "network." What are you doing to grow in knowledge so you can create value? What are you doing to expand your network? What are you doing to make sure people think of you when they need your product or service?

DAY 35
Prepare to Sell Your Lead Source on What You Can Bring to the Relationship

Once you have a meeting set up with a Wheel of the Fortunate lead partner for the first time, organize several pieces of information to get them interested in networking with you.

1. Be prepared to discuss several of your companies' larger clients (This list does not have to be exclusively your clients. The list can include *all of your companies'* larger clients).There's a good chance that a top sales professional might also be calling on the same clients and may have had little or no success getting business. The presumption is that you could introduce them into your network at the account and improve their position.

2. Be prepared to share a lead or two that may be news to them.

3. If your company purchases any type of industry information, lead information, demographic information, marketing information, bring that along. It's possible that your Wheel of the Fortunate lead partner might not have access to this type of information and may see great value in partnering with you simply to have access to the information.

4. Observe their responses to each of your offers. What you are looking for in a good partner is reciprocity. You want to see if they are willing to offer leads back to you. Perhaps you will jar their memory about large companies they are currently selling to that may be of interest to you. Maybe your leads will remind them of leads they have that you might not be aware of.

Finally, they may remember some of their companies' marketing information that might be helpful to you. With each exchange you are trying to see if they would be a good partner. Keep in mind that if they do not reciprocate during your first encounter, don't expect it to get any better. There are salespeople out there that don't understand the concept of reciprocity and these are not the salespeople you want in your networking group. However, if your research was correct and they are one of the top sales producers for their company they will take the information and run with it. They'll ask meaningful questions about your company, your sales process, and the like.

5. Be cautious, but honest. The goal is to determine if there's a fit and how or even if you want to proceed with the relationship. Remember, if it is not a good fit, you may be talking in the near future to another of their salespeople or to a salesperson who might be one of their competitors. Don't spill your beans until you see the connection!

DAY 36
Continue to Improve Your Lead Sharing Group

Make this a top priority to continue on a consistent basis: weekly, bi-weekly or at least once a month. Set a standing appointment and treat this just like an important customer because this process will drive more quality leads and opportunities your way than any other marketing or sales method!

Before you leave the first meeting make a follow-up date so you have a next step. There are three other ongoing expectations we believe you should set for this group to grow and provide more leads going forward.

1. Set a minimum number of leads you expect your lead partner to bring to every "meeting" (we put the word meeting in quotes because these lead exchange discussions could take place over the phone, via the web or face to face). This goes both ways so make sure you also meet or exceed this expectation.

2. Identify what lead sources are inappropriate. You don't want someone the night before the next meeting to read through the business section of the newspaper and bring in a lead that everyone knows about. At the same time, don't discount the fact that you may not have read the article. Set expectations of where they should come from but encourage discussion about information that is in the public domain.

3. Set a goal for how your Wheel of the Fortunate lead group is going to grow in size. Take the list of complimentary/noncompeting products/services from Day 29 and take the next two obvious categories; take one for

yourself and have the lead group take one. Set a deadline as to when each of you will identify the top provider and the top salesperson at the top provider from Days 30 and 31 and have an appointment to recruit another member of your Wheel of the Fortunate lead sharing group. When you do this you will double your group, from two to four. Once the two new members settle in repeat Days 30 and 31 again and you'll go from four to eight. Eight people appear to be an ideal size to remain clear on each person's business model and what they are looking for. Start another group on your own consisting of the products/services from Day 29 that are not in your first lead group and you'll begin to dominate your world of sales!

DAY 37
Qualification Criteria: Picking a Dance Partner

In an effort to be effective and efficient as a sales professional you will need to make sure you are dedicating your valuable time to qualified opportunities. This is a very difficult topic especially for new salespeople who are trying to prove themselves and feel they must focus on every prospect they hear about. Our approach is to identify the perfect prospect by developing a qualification criterion that can be used to compare and contrast each new opportunity. First, identify all the characteristics of the perfect customer. The best method to develop these characteristics is to simply list all of your company's good clients. This exercise may require you to interview existing salespeople from your company or your manager. If you are new and you have no predecessor to interview or you are starting your own company and have no existing customers then you will have to create the characteristics based on your existing knowledge. Given the fact that you've most likely made several sales, had several appointments and possibly closed several sales prior to today, you have some ideas of those characteristics that make a great client.

Here is a list of the characteristics that make our perfect client:

1. They have a budget that fits our price range.

2. They openly communicate their issues with us and answer our questions.

3. They are committed to training (they have either done training in the past or can explain why they want to do it now).

4. They will share whom they have used in the past and how it worked/issues they had.

5. They have more than five salespeople.

6. They have a desire to grow their people.

7. They have heard about us from another satisfied client/someone who has been through our training.

8. They can and are willing to explain how they are going to make the decision on training.

9. We know who the key decision maker is for the project.

There are other characteristics we look for such as fun to work with, major metropolitan area, willing to provide references, etc., and those are added to the list. Go ahead and make the list of the characteristics of your perfect client below. You can always add to the list at a later date. Another way to identify the positive characteristics is to list the negative characteristics that you've encountered along the way. List those negative characteristics and then take the opposite of each negative characteristic and create a list of the positive characteristics you desire.

Now, take the list of characteristics you've listed and write at least one question you could ask a prospect to identify whether they meet the criteria or not. You will be amazed how this will help you save time (efficiency) and help you focus on the highest probability sales opportunities.

At the same time it will equip you with great questions the first time you speak with a prospect. Once you draft your list of questions make sure to go back and make each of them open-ended (the prospect is unable to answer with a "yes" or a "no"). Use Who, What, When, Where, How or Why at the start of a question and it will typically be open ended and get the prospect talking and you learning!

Create your questions today!
(watch Video 151: Developing Great Questions on the Shot of Octane app)

DAY 38
When to Say "No:" The Other Side of Qualifying

You will learn to become more selective with whom you sell to over time. When you are new to a sales territory you will most likely work with prospects that are not as qualified because you fear passing an opportunity up. Your company may have given you the lead so you feel obligated or the prospect called you and was persistent about having you meet with them. There are many other reasons that cause us to invest our valuable time on opportunities that area poor use of our time and talents.

Take the questions you developed yesterday and put them down on paper. Organize them so the first question is the easiest to answer and the least challenging. Each subsequent question becomes a bit more direct. For instance, you may want to ask some questions about what they are currently using or if they have heard, or how they heard of your company before you get into the budget question. Frankly, these questions may result in a three-to-five-minute discussion so even though the budget question might be the most important to you it can become confrontational if asked too soon in the conversation.

We recommend taking your list of questions that are now organized as you would ask them and assign a simple rating to their importance. For instance, budget and willingness to share information is higher on the importance scale than if the prospect is located in a metropolitan area (using our criteria). If someone has the budget and they are sharing information, etc., that is more important to us than the fact they are located in an outlying area. By rating budget and willingness to share information as more important than the prospect's location, it helps keep priorities straight. As a result, you can make a good decision relative to the other opportunities you have in front of you and in terms of the leads you are chasing.

Make the effort today to identify those key characteristics of your ideal customer, assign a "weight/priority" to each characteristic and develop questions to identify the prospect's fit with each characteristic. Now you not only have a great way to ask questions early in your relationship with a potential customer, but also a way to determine how qualified the prospect is and their priority relative to your other opportunities.

DAY 39
Who Takes the Lead?

There are several different approaches to Prospecting and they are derived from the source of the "Lead" ("Lead" defined as a company or individual whom you decide to pursue in an effort to qualify, sell and bring value). The priority of the lead will depend on how you classify the lead, hence the title for today, "Who Takes the Lead?"

With the Sales Continuum approach we classify a Lead one off our ways. Each classification will determine the strategy, script and marketing approach we take. The four classifications are Referral lead, Warm lead, Target lead, and Cold lead.

Referral Lead – In some cases you will "Prospect" to a referral. When someone who is aware of the product or service you sell gives you the name of a company or person who they feel would benefit from your product or service, *and they have specific information such as stated need, budget, timeline, etc.,* that lead becomes a Referral lead. Referral leads can come from existing or past customers, friends, association members, and others. In some cases the Referral lead will be for an opportunity within an existing customer for another division. Referral leads are extremely important which is why we put them first on our list. Now and in the future the technologies that "block" you from getting through to a prospect will continue to make it more difficult for you to connect with a prospect. Having a referral is key as it may be the difference between a prospect deleting your "prospecting" message or taking your call.

Warm Lead – In some cases you will Prospect a company or individual because they have a need or situation you believe your product or service can address. Oftentimes these Warm leads come from people who know something about your product/service and want to help you out. The Warm lead is different from the Referral

Lead even though it may come from an existing customer. The key difference is that *you do not have* information such as the specific need, a specific timeline or specific funding/budget or that the person who is providing you with the Warm lead has not spoken to or has any personal/business connection to the Warm lead. While Warm leads are better than cold leads they are not as valuable as a Referral lead. In many cases we don't have the personal connection with the Warm lead. We don't have a common name to try to warm up our phone calls or e-mails.

Target Lead – As noted on Day 9 the Target lead is someone from our Wish 100 list.

Cold Lead – In many cases you may not have access to referrals or your company may not provide Warm leads, or qualified target accounts for you to Prospect. You may have been handed a phonebook or a similar list of contacts/companies, which you know very little about (beyond the phone number…and that may even be wrong!). The Sales Continuum is set up to handle all four levels of a prospect (Target, Referral, Warm lead, and Cold lead). The key is taking those initial customers and converting them into another list of Referrals or at least Warm leads from which you can prospect.

That's the key!

From time to time there will be crossover between these different prospect categories. In some cases you may be calling on someone who was given to you as a Referral lead and you also have the mon your Target list. With the Sales Continuum system we always take the *highest probability* prospect category that applies when labeling the prospect. Referral lead trumps Warm lead; Warm lead trumps Target lead; and Target lead trumps Cold lead. It's important to keep the classification of your leads up to date as you always want to be working the highest probability leads. While it may seem to be self-evident, the reality is that oftentimes we tend to put higher probability leads to the side because of our fear of rejection or fear of failure. The sales professional will call on the highest probability opportunities which have the greatest chance to succeed thereby increasing their self-confidence.

Take your list of prospects and categorize them as either a Referral, Warm, Target or Cold lead. You may have existing customers from Day 9; remember that your existing contact list is one of the best resources you have to start with. Take your "Wish 100" companies/contacts from Day 9, or lists of contacts/companies from your employer. Take all of these lists and identify each Prospect as R (Referral), W (Warm), T (Target) or C (Cold).

DAY 40
Sales Octane Mantra #11—Don't Let Investigation Become Procrastination!

One of the common fears of salespeople is the fear of rejection. We fear the prospect might say they are not interested (rejection!) so we don't make the call. It's typical at this stage of the process to spend a lot of time investigating your list of contacts and leads to make sure everything is perfect. Unfortunately this investigation often is just an excuse for procrastination driven by our fear of rejection. Don't let this become the case with you! Set an aggressive goal of how much time (start time, stop time) you are going to spend investigating your leads and stick to it. Make the call as soon as you reach the stop time — there are no excuses! What you'll find is the fear of rejection is always greater than the occurrence of rejection. By setting an aggressive goal and making the call you will begin to build your self-confidence and minimize your fear.

DAY 41
Sales Octane Mantra #12— Integrity Is Doing What You Say You Will Do and Doing What Is Right

Information travels faster today than at any point in history. This statement will not change as we will continue to invent ways to communicate at lightning speed. That is why the sales professional must understand the importance of having integrity! Much has been written about integrity. For the sales professional it means two things, doing what you say you will do and doing what is right. To the extent you do what you say you will do and do what is right you will be known as a person of integrity. Think of this as the Integrity bank account. Every time you do what you say you will door do what is right you make a deposit into the Integrity bank account with your clients. Every time you fail to do something you said you would do or fail to do the right thing you make a withdrawal from the Integrity bank account with your clients. There is one major difference between a traditional bank account and the Integrity bank account. A deposit and withdrawal do not have the same value. One small withdrawal can evaporate a large deposit if not bankrupt your account!

With many prospective customers you will need to make many deposits in the Integrity bank account before they will even talk to you. Clients tend to forget all the good things you do for them but never forget when you fail to deliver on a commitment. This reality demands that we make our commitments carefully ("I'll give you a call tomorrow") and then do what we say we will do. The statement "Do what is right" might appear to be open to a values judgment. It's not. You know when you are doing the client "right" and you know when you're not. Information travels and your reputation will follow you wherever you go. Make a commitment to do what you say you will do and do what is right.

DAY 42
What Is So Compelling About Your Product or Service?

Before you make the call you want to understand something about the prospect and a key value offered by your product/service. The key is to put yourself in a position to secure an appointment either over the phone or face to face. You need to invest some time, more or less depending on your industry and the size of your sale, to uncover one or two items from the prospect's current situation that you can connect with the key advantages you offer. This may feel like a lot of work the first time you run through this step. However, as the weeks and months go by you will identify several circumstances or situations with prospective customers that keep surfacing during your sales calls.

Many of these circumstances or situations are often simple to identify from the resources noted in Day 43. For example, let's say you sell dental supplies to dental offices and one of your key advantages is you provide the largest breadth of dental products compared to others in the dental supply industry. Let's say this is viewed as an advantage by many existing clients, especially dentists who have aligned themselves together into a group to improve their size, geographic coverage, and buying power. As a result, the characteristic or situation we are looking for with regard to prospective dentists is dentists that are part of a large group or association. If we can identify dentists with this characteristic or situation then we have something to connect their situation with our key advantage and this becomes our leverage point for the appointment. Let's do another example. Let's say you are selling MRO supplies, a basic commodity sale with numerous competitors. One of your key advantages is an online order status capability so your clients can quickly check the status of their order. The characteristic or situation that many of your current clients have is they have so many MRO items they purchase. The MRO person is constantly being hounded by the department that's waiting for the "part," so your ability to quickly share online the status without having to track down the MRO salesperson is very beneficial. Subsequently, the characteristic or current situation we are looking for are companies with a MRO buyer who is accountable for multiple locations and a lot of individual purchases! We'll take these examples through the next step so you can see how to use this connection.

Customers buy for personal and emotional reasons and then justify their decision based on facts and figures. The "hook" you will use to secure an appointment is key when making cold calls. Even referral calls benefit from a compelling "hook." This sound bite must make a personal or emotional connection with the prospect and get them to listen to your message, take your call or return your call. What are some of the personal and emotional reasons people decide to invest with you or other manufacturers that compete with you? Is it to save money, increase productivity, improve safety/compliance, save space, increase speed, decrease maintenance, increase sales? What is it? Once you have that list of key values and you've investigated the prospect to see where the connection point might be, then you can put together a tight sound-bite.

DAY 43
Warming Up the Cold Call

Before you pick up the phone take a look at a couple of resources that might help you better position your cold call and "warm up" the lead. The first place you should go is to your prospect's website. There is typically a lot of information that you can use to make your "connection." Look at the mission statement for some insight into the companies' culture. Look for a key business issue that is important to them and also a good connection for your company, your product or your service. Look for new initiatives, which you can reference and provide positive reinforcement ("With your new XYZ product line it's clear that your company is well positioned for growth"). Look for points of connection between your initiatives and their initiatives.

Their job postings/career opportunities are a good indication of whether they are in a growth mode or in a decline mode. While you are at the career/job postings site be on the look out for the prospect's e-mail extension and their e-mail "logic." Do they put the last name first, abbreviate the letter of an employee's first name (For example, first name of the individual and @salesoctane.com)? If they have the names and e-mails of employees (this is very rare) then you've hit the jackpot. If not, then take note of the e-mail logic and extension (example, @Salesoctane.com) which will be helpful later in this process.

Next, take the key values you offer from Day 43 and look for similar connection points. If your product increases productivity then look for an indication that the prospect is driving toward increased productivity. If you improve safety, look for references to the importance of safety. Any connection you can make between their stated initiatives and your capabilities will be helpful when approaching the prospect.

Look at other websites. As of this writing, there is no shortage of new websites that serve as great resources. Let me list a few general categories:

1. Fee based Business Reports – If you put the words "Business Reports" in your search engine you will find several excellent fee-based business reporting tools available. For a nominal fee you can search private and public companies for valuable information. Check with your Sales Manager to see if your company already has a license. Whoever completes your customer credit evaluations at your company may already subscribe to one of these services for gathering financial information. You may be able to use that license to gather information valuable to your selling effort.

2. The prospect's industry association – If you take the general product or service category, go to one of the major search engines, and plug in the name of the product or service category and the words "trade association" (For example, office furniture, trade association). You will get a number of websites that speak to the industry of your prospect.

   The key here is to look through several of these websites and search for some clues about possible changes in your prospect's world that might connect to your top value. This may include changes in regulations, industry growth/decline, problems/issues, etc. You are looking for a topic that is key to their industry that may have a connection with *your* product or service.

3. Clipping service – There are several cost-effective resources that provide you with articles where your prospect's name (company, person, etc.) has appeared. This is often an excellent connection point as the topic of the article may be something you can spin with your point of connection. If nothing else, you can send a note with the article congratulating the prospect and noting that you will be contacting them shortly. It may take a while to secure a quality appointment, and a sustained marketing effort that leverages occasional newspaper articles may be the difference!

4. The "front desk" – In many cases you can identify some or all of what you are looking for by asking some brief questions of the front desk personnel. This is most likely over the phone; however, this can also be done face to face if you are physically working a geographic area. Keep in mind the front desk is often extremely busy with incoming calls and other work. Do not waste their time.

Using a Letter of Introduction

Another way to warm up the call is to send the prospect a letter of introduction either via snail mail or e-mail. This letter states that you will be contacting them on a particular day and why you are calling. You can use information from today's research to make the connection between their company and your capabilities. A great way to capture their attention is to use a quote from a satisfied customer and include that in bold font at the top of your letter, especially if it's someone they have heard of or someone from their industry. The last step in the Sales Continuum is to ask your customer for a letter of reference (Day 95). Take excerpts from the letters of reference and use them in this letter of introduction.

Now you have information that can be used to warm up the call! Take the time to do some research on a few of your leads to identify some key points of interest before making the call.

DAY 44
Developing Trust with the First Phone Call

Now it's time to develop your voice mail/conversation approach for the first call. Let's start with the introduction which is key! We estimate that decision makers listen to a voice mail approximately eight to ten seconds before they begin to multi-task and lose interest in your message. The prospect will listen to approximately the first eight to ten seconds and either outright press the delete button (because it is obviously a salesperson and they don't want to be bothered) or they will start checking their e-mail, opening their snail mail, looking through some paperwork, or some other innocuous task, but they certainly are not focused on your message. Based on the importance of those first eight to ten seconds we have to avoid spewing unimportant information (like how long your company has been in business, a detailed description of all the products and services you offer, where you are located, etc.).

Sales Octane approaches the cold call and referral call the same way. We start with, "Good Morning, Mr. Jones, this is (your first and last name) from (your company)." Keep in mind that if your company uses an acronym and the extended version spelled out, it will be extremely lengthy. Unless your extended company name has great brand recognition, why would you waste the most valuable first impression spewing the name of the company when it has no brand recognition? Get to the fact that someone has referred you or that another company similar to them recently purchased from you and those customers are getting a particular value!

If you are dealing with a referral then begin with "Good Morning, Mr. Jones, (Referrer's first and last name) recommended I give you a call. This is (your first and last name) from (your company)."

The next line is equally as important for maintaining their interest. Many sales books talk about using an elegant line of prose about your product/service, what they do, the value they bring, and/or anything which will raise eyebrows. However, the typical eyebrow is raised in suspicion because it sounds either too good to be true or it sounds like a sales line used by a desperate salesperson. The approach of the Sales Continuum is to develop a trust factor by informing the prospect we are doing business and bringing value to other people — just like them — who are in a similar situation. We do this for two reasons. First, over 50 percent of the population is automatically suspicious of any sales proposition that comes out of your mouth. This is based on their behavioral style; it's the way they are wired and you are not going to change them.

As a matter of fact, if you try to change the way they process information you will lose them and the sale. They want to know that what you are selling has been used by someone else and they are probably going to want to talk to them to confirm that what you are saying is accurate. The other 50 percent of the population is also interested in the fact that someone else has used your product. Their interest, however, is not in avoiding risk. Their interest is in who you've done business with and if those customers are cutting-edge, someone they know or someone they wish to emulate. The bottom line is everyone, regardless of their situation, wants to know that you have successfully done business with others similar to them! We recommend using the sound-bite "similar to you," combined with the very top-line value your existing "customer" has experienced with your product or service. When you do this, you remove some of the resistance by decreasing the suspicion and/or raising interest.

Here are a few examples based on the value issues raised on Day 43.

Without the referral – "Good morning Dr. Jones, this is Bob Smith from ABC Dental Supply. We recently finished a project with a Dental Group 'similar to you' and they were able to increase their efficiency by 30%."

With a referral – "Good Morning, Dr. Jones, Dr. Porter recommended I give you a call. This is Bob Smith from ABC Dental Supply. We just recently finished a project with Dr. Porters group and they were able to increase their efficiency by 30%."

Now tell them what you want! Most prospects are busy and don't have time to sit back and listen to you drone on. Most prospects will at least listen to this next statement given the fact that you used a reference name *or* because you noted that you've done business with someone similar to them and you brought value. So tell them what you want. Is it an appointment, an online demonstration, a phone call? Let's say we want an appointment (anything you decide will fit into this process). Be clear and concise, "I'd like to schedule a brief appointment" then add a very, very (did I say *very*) top-level statement of what you will do during that appointment. Make sure to include what you would like from them (they come first), how you plan to build credibility for your product/service and finally, some disclaimer that if they don't want what you have to offer you'll go away. For example, "I'd like to schedule a brief appointment to learn more about your new project, share some specifics of some recent projects we've done and then you can decide if this might work for you."

Now, let's run it from the top without a Referral – "Good Morning, Dr. Jones, this is Bob Smith from ABC Dental Supply, we recently finished a project with a Dental Group similar to yours and they were able to increase their efficiency by 30%." I'd like to schedule a brief appointment to learn more about your new project, share some specifics of some recent projects we've done and then you can decide if this might work for you."

We're getting near the end. Now that you've told them what you'd like, now tell them what you're going to do. Too often salespeople tell their prospects what to do with statements like "Why don't you give me a call," or "Why don't you give me a call back at 800 IAM POOR." Or, if you're really slick you'll say "Please call me back at your earliest convenience at 800 IAM LAME." The last time I checked *you* were the salesperson (the pursuer) and they are the prospect (the pursued). So why are you leaving it up to them to call you back? If they don't call you back does that mean they are not interested? If they don't call you back *how long can you wait* before you call them again *without looking desperate?* The key here is to tell them specifically what you are going to do next *and* offer them the opportunity to call you if they would like. For example, "I'll give you a call next Thursday, the 22nd, or, if there's a better time feel free to give me a call at 800 IAM GOOD, again, 800 IAM GOOD!" I recommend leaving your number twice at the end of the voice mail message simply because most people do not listen to their voice mail with a pen in their hand waiting to write your message down. By leaving your number twice, and slowing down when you repeat your number the second time, you will give them adequate time to get the number (and they will like you more!).

Leave it positive! At the end of the message put something in that is positive. It could be "Thanks and have a great weekend" or "Thanks and I look forward to speaking with you" or "Thanks, I look forward to meeting you" etc.

Type your prospecting script from today's material and practice it *out loud* throughout the day. Make changes to areas that are uncomfortable for you but don't remove any of the key components. In a few days you'll be ready to go live on the phone.

Note: We do not recommend leaving your telephone number at the beginning of the message. Your prospect only pays attention for the first several seconds and if they suspect you are a salesperson they'll probably delete your message before you've ever gotten to a referral name, what you've done for others or the fact that people just like them are buying from you every single day!

DAY 45
Finding the Right Voice for Cold Calling

Whether you are cold calling over the phone or face to face (walking into offices without an appointment), your voice and how you project yourself visually are extremely important. Albert Mehrabian studied the impact of words a person uses, the voice a person uses and a person's visual characteristics and how much of the message is retained by the receiving party. The words you use represent 7 percent, your vocal inflection, how your voice sounds and how you inflect your voice represents 38 percent, and how you appear visually represents 55 percent. Clearly how you appear visually is important. This is not a book on how to groom and dress but there are plenty of sources for that information and they are worth your investment of time and money. Just know that your visuals have a tremendous impact, literally dwarfing the words you say! Salespeople often stay up late the night before a sales call reviewing the words they are going to say but seldom realize that how they say it (their vocal inflection) and their visual presence, use of body language, and visual media will often win or lose the sale. For the purposes of today's material we are going to focus solely on how you use this knowledge when making phone calls.

First, you need to set the benchmark by listening to yourself using a script for your product/service (your cold-call script) from Day 44. You can use a recorder, your voice message system or even your video recorder but you must have a benchmark. After you listen to it write down your comments. Do you talk fast? Do you drone on? Does your message have a direction or are you scurrying all over the place? Do you say *um*, and *ahh*? Do you sound positive or negative? Do you sound desperate or confident?

Here are some ideas to improve your voice and vocal inflection.

First, recognize that your brain works much faster than your mouth. Your brain is way ahead of your mouth and that can cause problems. That's where the *ahh* and *um* comes from; that's where talking too fast comes from and that's where talking without a direction originates. Be more confident and let your brain organize your thoughts *before* you open your mouth. *Slow down!* "And ahh, and um" is simply the brain saying "you're not saying anything, you don't know what to say dummy, *say something!*" and out it comes, "So ahh, I'd like to um say that ahh…" and in fact your brain was right, you sound dumb. Instead slow down and think of what you're going to say before you say it and record yourself again. Literally, say everything in your mind, before you say it out loud. You will be amazed at how your speech is paced—there is a clear direction to your words, and you sound confident!

Next, try to go up at the end of certain words versus consistently going down at the end of words and statements. This takes some practice. When you listen to your recording you will notice that even though you are more paced and clear when slowing down and using a script, there may be a lack of confidence and emotion. Take the script you developed and look at points where you could go up at the end of a word or statement to make your voice sound more positive and confident. The easiest is the very last statement in your script. Most of the time when someone says, "Thanks and have a good day," it would appear they were greeting you in a line at the funeral home. It sounds like an afterthought and there's little, if any, positive emotion. Don't get me wrong. I'm not saying you should sound like a cheerleader (those voicemail endings are somewhat obnoxious) but find a pleasant and positive approach to wishing someone a good day and make it sound like you mean it. You should also sound presumptuous.

Here's what I mean by presumptuous. You need to share that people are buying from you (even if this is your first day on the job and you've not made one sale). One way to do that is to use statements like "I'm going to be tied up through this Friday with clients, so I will get back to you on the 16th." This is a good statement to use right before you tell them what *you're going to do!* Subsequent calls and conversations should always include something to show that customers are buying from you. This is a major improvement over "I'll be in all week so give me a call anytime." Occasionally a participant in one of our workshops will raise concern that reinforcing you are busy may be a turn-off to prospective customers who will expect your total and complete attention. They questioned whether the prospective customer will be concerned that your busy schedule will get in the way of their needs. This is a good point. Our approach is to always make the follow-up call and meet follow-up commitments *when we said we would*. That integrity will reinforce that we do what we say we will do and we will meet their needs. If you are reinforcing you are busy with clients, and then miss a follow-up date or commitment then, yes, this approach will backfire.

Before you make your prospecting calls make sure to look at your calendar and know when you will tell them you will follow up. Have that date in front of you so you can say, with confidence, "I'm going to be tied up through this Friday with appointments, so I will get back to you on Monday the 27th" and you know you will!

Continue to practice your script and add the voice inflection to sound positive, reinforcing, confident, and that you are busy helping clients with your products and services.

DAY 46
Making the Call: Embracing the Gatekeeper Even if You Have a Contact Name

Now that you have a basic script, and you know what you want (appointment/demonstration/plant tour, etc.) it's time to make the phone call.

If you have name of the contact

If you have the name of the person you need to speak with we still recommend calling through the receptionist or administrative assistant (gatekeeper). People buy from people they like. This is a basic fundamental of selling. If you can expand your contacts within an account and get more contacts to like you, you will win more often. The gatekeeper can be a difficult but thankless job. There are very few calls they answer that they would identify as "enjoyable." You can change that. The talking points noted today are positioned to get them to like you, or at a minimum accept you, so you obtain the information you need and are better positioned to achieve your goals. Here's an example of how to approach the gatekeeper:

"Good morning, I'm (first name, last name) from (company name). Thanks for taking my call. Would you be kind enough to connect me to (contact's first and last name) voice mail or are they in right now? Thanks, have a good day." Don't forget your sincere and positive voice inflection from Day 45.

Note: If the gatekeeper asks what this is about provide a concise statement and respond in a positive, presumptuous, "matter of fact" manner. Keep in mind that most salespeople "give away" their lack of confidence when making cold calls *and* the gatekeeper is very good at responding back with "we're not interested right now," or

"Ms. Jones is not taking vendor calls" or some other attempt to shut you down. It's very difficult to call back and get around the gatekeeper once they've shut you down. Sound positive and presumptuous like they are expecting your call and *of course they want to talk to you!*

If after your second or third attempt you are still not connected to your prospect then it's appropriate to circle back with the gatekeeper (whom you left with a positive feeling) and say, "I've left Sally Jones several messages already. It sounds like she's busy, if you were me, when would you call?" The intent of this question is to give power to the gatekeeper, which they appreciate, and allow them to lead you to the best strategy to connect with your prospect.

Oftentimes the receptionist/gatekeeper is aware of the best time to reach the prospect/contact. Regardless of their response, thank them and when you finally connect with the contact make sure to circle back and thank the gatekeeper. They are often the key to additional contacts going forward.

If you don't have the contact's name

You: Good morning, I'm (first name, last name) from (company name), thanks for taking my call. (By thanking them sincerely you position yourself in a positive light).

You: Who am I speaking with?

Gatekeeper: (They will typically give you their First or First &Last Name)

You: (Say their First Name Only), I need your help (Say this in a sincere manner which should be easy because when you think about it...you do! The goal is to put them in a position of power or authority over you. By informing them that you "need their help" you place them in a position where they may want to help you more than if you had just asked the next question.

You: I help companies with their (Your Product/Service). Who makes the decisions regarding (Your Product/Service) your company? (State your Product/Service in terms of what you do as generally as possible. This is not the time to go into a lengthy discussion of all the details of your products and services.)

Gatekeeper: Oh, that would be Sally Jones in Finance.

You: How do you spell (Last/First name)?

You: So I don't have to keep calling you, what is Ms. Jones direct number? (Always ask this question since once you get into your prospecting campaign it's best to call before and after business hours and even during the lunch to get them on the phone. At the same time, calling early in the morning and after business hours, sends the message you are working hard and are a busy person which translates to "people are buying from me." Second, by offering the "win" for the receptionist/gatekeeper "don't have to keep bothering you" you increase the probability of them giving you this information.)

You: Oh, one last question, I need to send her an e-mail is it *jones@xxxxxx.com*? (Remember in Day 44 during your research we said to identify the prospect's e-mail logic? This is where you use that information. By using the e-mail logic during this question the presumption is you are already aware of the information and you are simply confirming the e-mail. Finally, by using the statement "oh, one last thing" you are putting them on notice that this is the last question you are going to ask and since they are probably getting near the point where the lights are flashing on the telephone console...they will give you the information given the fact this is your last question.)

You: Thanks so much, would you be kind enough to connect me to (Contact's First & Last Name) voice mail or are they in right now? (Always finish by thanking them. It pairs you with a positive and leaves them with a positive impression.)
That's it! You now have a time-honored approach to find the names of the contacts at target companies and positively influence the gatekeeper for future connections.

DAY 47
Sales Octane Mantra #13—You Often Get Kicked Down, but You Hardly Ever Get Kicked Up. Start High in the Organization!

One of the opportunities I see sales people routinely miss is going in at a higher level. This is either because:

- They do not feel worthy of calling higher in the organization. This is typically caused by a lack of confidence.

- They have routinely called on a particular "title" that is lower in the organization and they've not thought of going in at a higher level. This is typically because they have fallen into a routine.

- They don't believe their product would be of interest to those in higher positions of a company. This is brought on by not truly understanding the benefits their product/service brings to their clients.

- They have been summarily rejected by the higher levels whenever they have tried in the past. While this is their reality...seldom, if ever, is there a track record of this type of rejection. They tried a few times, it did not work, the rejection hurt and they stopped.

- If you have experienced other reasons not included in our list please forward them to us at *www.salesoctane.com*

Whatever your reason for starting low on the organization chart I want to challenge you to lift your sights. Many top-level contacts will, in fact, kick you down a level or two in the organization. Often these meetings with a top-level contact will be brief and they will direct you to another contact. Why, then, should you start higher in the organization if you're going to get kicked down anyway? The reason is that once you've spoken to someone at a higher level in an organization, you have an "introduction" to other contacts. This is an excellent sales strategy for two reasons:

- Since the next contact is typically lower in the organization, the fact that you have been "referred" by someone higher up the organization chart sends a positive message. The perception may be that you have a connection to the higher level contact or that the higher level contact liked what you shared with them. In either case, you come to the next appointment in a stronger position.

- Every time you go in at a higher level you always learn something you did not know about the prospect's company, their team or their product. This information will help you further qualify them as a target, identify additional ways to sell their account or in some cases even uncover additional contacts. Oftentimes you will hear about their customers and their suppliers both of which could be potential new sales contacts for you. You always get something out of a meeting with a top level decision maker!

Here is one last point about going in higher in the organization. If they want to "kick you down" to another contact don't simply get the name, say thanks and leave. Instead, ask them if they would be able to make the introduction for you. If they can't, then ask them if they would be willing to let the person know you will be calling. Obviously the person could either e-mail or leave a message or even have their administrative assistant take care of those details. The key is that the new contact knows the fact that their leader has recommended *you* call *them!*

Take a few minutes right now and look at several of your target accounts and make a commitment to identify a top-level decision maker and start there! You'll probably get kicked down but you'll learn additional information, uncover additional prospects both within the target company and possibly outside the company and position yourself to go to the lower level contact with a reinforcing start to your sales call. This will definitely increase your self-confidence!

Note: this technique is to be used when starting the prospecting process. It is dangerous to go back in at a higher level if you've already had the door shut at the lower level. You can certainly try this direction if you have no other option; however, "going over the head" of a contact after they've shut the door is a risky strategy. Go in higher at the start!

DAY 48
Sales Octane Mantra #14—Creating the ZONE for Prospecting

As you prepare to prospect, we recommend establishing a time and a physical environment when making your calls. This puts you in the ZONE for prospecting. This weekend think about when and where you should make your prospecting calls.

Time – Too often salespeople try to "get to" or "fit in" their phone prospecting. Most salespeople have an aversion to phone prospecting because of the probability of rejection. As a result they avoid phone prospecting by not carving out a specific time in their calendar. There are a few reasons you want to set aside a specific timeframe to make all your prospecting calls.

- You can have your research, scripts, telephone numbers and contact management software on your computer screen in front of you and run through the list in a very efficient manner.

- By making several calls in a row you will notice your confidence increasing after you get over the first one or two calls.

- With proper planning you can use a space where others will not listen to you or distract you during these important calls. You can reserve a conference room, enclosed office or make the calls from your home.

- You will have your calendar in front of you to select the day when you will be calling them next.

- There may be a specific time when you have a higher probability of connecting with prospects. If that's the case then you need to take this into consideration.

- You may have more energy or the right frame of mind at onetime versus another time during the day. Take this into consideration when planning your Prospecting time.

Based on your results from the exercise on Day 11 you most likely know how many calls you need to make on a weekly and daily basis. This should help set the number of days and hours within the day you must set aside to make prospecting calls.

Physical location – It is common practice for underperforming salespeople to seek out sales professionals who are making prospecting calls and taunt them. They wait to hear the confident sales professional making call after call and they look over the cubicle and make some cynical remark. And while there are many options to minimize this distraction, the best advice is to make your prospecting calls behind closed doors. Literally find a conference room or office where you can close the door or make the calls from your home. This way you can sound confident, presumptuous, and like everyone is buying from you (even if you have just started) and no one is going to know the difference.

You should have a headset so your hands are free to make notes or work the contact management program on your computer. Given the fact that the Prospect can't visually see you, use hand gestures and movement to punctuate your statements over the phone. These physical dynamics will impact your vocal inflection in a positive manner. If possible, stand up as your motion and movement will create emotion in your voice.

Figure out when and where you will make your prospecting calls (a specific start and stop time). Now you have a plan as you start the week!

DAY 49
Mental Preparation to Improve Your Prospecting

Having the right mindset going into your prospecting calls is essential. The following are several steps you can take to improve your prospecting experience:

- Motivation – Most salespeople have something driving them toward their sales goal. There is typically something greater than simply attaining their sales goal. It could be providing for their family, maybe something they wish to purchase, for a vacation they wish to take. Identify one or more motivations that drive you toward your goal and create a visual reminder for each. This could be as simple as a picture of your family, or the item you wish to purchase or the location you wish to visit. Keep these images in front of you (literally) when making your prospecting calls. Since most salespeople are visual learners these pictures will serve as a visual reminder of your goal and motivate you through your calls.

- Confidence – You sound better when you are confident. Your stress is reduced and that translates into a smooth, confident, presumptuous approach. If you talk to top-sales professionals or if you've had success with selling you know the best time to sell is when you've just sold something. While many salespeople go back to the office, or home, or somewhere else to celebrate their sale, the sales professional gets on the phone and makes calls to prospective accounts. Why? Because the confidence from the recent sale puts them in a zone where the next prospect picks up their confidence and presumes this is someone who is best in class. The key is to create that same level of confidence every time you pick up the phone. If you see yourself as a sales professional, having just closed a huge sale, the brain cannot distinguish between your thoughts and reality. See yourself as the top-sales professional in your product/service arena. Think of several positive sales situations you've been in and visually see yourself in those situations prior to picking up the phone. Go back to Day 45and make sure you are using the positive, confident voice inflection we spoke about.

- Visualize – Most salespeople are visual learners (when compared to auditory learners or kinesthetic learners). Prior to picking up the phone you need to visualize the motivation pictures. Prior to picking up the phone you need to visualize confident selling situations. Prior to picking up the phone you need to visualize the call going very, very well. Whatever your goals are for the call, you need to visualize the successful achievement of each of those goals. Visualizing success will put you in the right frame of mind for the call!

DAY 50
Run Next Door: Face-to-Face Cold Prospecting Calls

If you have a sales role that requires you to go from prospect company to prospect company and basically knock on doors versus making phone calls then this step is for you. Even if you seldom make face-to-face cold prospecting calls we recommend that whenever you are in the field it makes sense to stop by and knock on a few doors. There's nothing better than to go into an office, walk up to the receptionist and reference the fact that you are working with a company next door. It's instant credibility. There's also a good chance the receptionist may even know someone at that company which makes you even more reputable.

We recommend using the same approach as Day 46 with the following modification. When you walk up to the receptionist, introduce yourself and immediately state that you *do not have an appointment*. This does two things: it confirms your honesty and disarms the receptionist. The receptionist will appreciate your honesty. Also, the receptionist is most likely going to ask if you have an appointment anyway and then follow up with a few additional negatives such as, "We don't see vendors without an appointment" or "Leave your card and if we're interested we'll give you a call" (and you will probably never get that call). In both cases you are on your heels and they are in control. Instead follow this approach:

You: (Extending your business card) Good morning, I'm Jim Ryerson from Sales Octane. I don't have an appointment today, but I need your help. We help companies with their Sales Training. Who makes the decisions regarding Sales Training for your company? (State your Product/Service in terms of what you do as generally as possible. This is not the time to go into a lengthy discussion of all the details of your products and services. Instead, you are trying to identify the key, top-level decision maker. Select a product or service description that most everyone will understand.)

Gatekeeper: Oh, that would be Sally Jones in Sales.

You: How do you spell (Last/First Name)? (This is in case there is any question in your mind how to spell their name since you will need it later for e-mail or direct mail.)

You: So I don't have to bother you in the future, what is Ms. Jones direct number?

You: Oh, one last question, I need to send her an e-mail, it is *sjones@XYZ.com*? (which you found on Day 43)

You: Thanks so much, could I leave a message for Sally in her voice mail or is she in right now?

Note: An alternative is after you ask for the name of the person who makes the decisions around your product/service is to reference the fact that you gave the receptionist your card and ask them if you can have the decision maker's card. In some cases they will give you the card and in other cases they won't. If they don't, then go down the path of asking for the correct spelling, direct telephone number and e-mail address.

You now have an approach for a cold call when you have a name, when you don't have a name and when you are making a face to face cold call. Practice this technique today in conjunction with another appointment or simply leave your office and go next door to try out the technique. It's easy once you have the words!

DAY 51
They Did Not Return Your Call?
Surprised? Time to Become Very
Persistent!

Other than referral calls, few initial voicemails ever prompt a return call in the prospecting world. The reason is not because you did a poor job. More often than not it has to do with the fact that the prospect is busier than they've ever been before. Even with all the efficiency improvement tools at our disposal, we are busier than we've ever been. In addition, information is readily available to the masses and there are more sales people clogging up their voicemail. The key becomes your persistence! Your voicemail message (if you followed the talking points) clearly stated when *you* would call them back. Remember Sales Octane Mantra #12 from Day 42? Integrity is doing what you say you will do and doing what's right. So do what you say you will do and make another call. Studies indicate that sales people make an average of two calls before they give up. Think about that! We recommend between two to three voicemail messages just so the prospect can hear:

- Your confident voice

- The fact you are busy ("I'm going to be tied up with customers for the next couple of days")

- Your professional approach

- The fact that other people similar to them are using your services.

We do all of this so the prospect will conclude you are a good person. And by doing what you said you were going to do you have made deposits into the Integrity Bank Account and sent the message you are persistent. Would you want to give your time, attention and money to a salesperson who does not follow through? And don't you think you're a rational, thoughtful person? So why give up on a prospect? Why even get upset with the fact they've not returned your call? They are simply checking to see if you follow through, if you have integrity, if you are persistent and if they can count on you.

The second message is a shorter variation of the talking points from Day 44.

Without referral – "Good Morning, Mr. Jones, this is Bob Smith from ABC Company, I'm sorry we keep missing each other. I'm going to be tied up through this (day of the week/date) with clients/appointments/projects, so I'll give you a call next Thursday, the 22nd, or, if it's more convenient/if there's a better time feel free to give me a call at 800 IAM GOOD, again, 800 IAM GOOD! Thanks and have a great day."

With a referral – "Good Morning, Mr. Jones, Sue Porter recommended I give you a call. My name is Bob Smith from ABC Company. I'm sorry we keep missing each other. I'm going to be tied up through this (day of the week/date) with clients/appointments/projects, so I'll give you a call next Thursday, the 22nd, or, if it's more convenient/if there's a better time feel free to give me a call at 800 IAM GOOD, again, 800 IAM GOOD!"

The third call is modified *if* you have their e-mail.

Without referral/With e-mail address – "Good Morning, Mr. Jones, this is Bob Smith from ABC Company, I'm sorry we keep missing each other. It sounds like you're busy so in case it's easier for you to reply I think I'll just send you an e-mail. Then I'll give you a call next Thursday, the 22nd, or, as always, feel free to give me a call at 800 IAM GOOD, again, 800 IAM GOOD! Thanks and have a great day."

With a referral – "Good Morning, Mr. Jones, Sue Porter recommended I give you a call. My name is Bob Smith from ABC Company. I'm sorry we keep missing each other. It sounds like you're busy so in case it's easier for you to reply I think I'll just send you an e-mail. Then I'll give you a call next Thursday, the 22nd, or, as always, feel free to give me a call at 800 IAM GOOD, again, 800 IAM GOOD! Thanks and have a great day."

The e-mail should be short and sweet with no attachments. Most spam filters will snag your email if you have too many attachments. The best information to put in the e-mail is the talking points you left in the first voicemail.

In the subject line of the e-mail put something very similar to the start of your voicemail.

Example 1 – Subject: Jim Ryerson, Sales Octane, June Smith recommended I follow up with you.

Example 2 – Subject: Jim Ryerson, Sales Octane, following up as promised.

The goal of the e-mail is not to sell them but to get them to connect with you. By keeping the talking points the same you improve the chance that they will make the connection between the positive, confident, busy person who is calling them and your e-mail.

Be prepared, you will typically get a response to an e-mail far faster than a voice- mail! However, if you're thinking that maybe you should simply start with e-mails and forego the phone calls think again. You want to make the calls so they can **hear** how positive and confident you are. You want to make the calls to **show** how organized and responsible you are. You want to make the calls because it shows you follow through and do what you
say you will do!

Never give up!

DAY 52
They Answered!

While this is becoming less and less the case, occasionally the prospect does answer the phone. Many salespeople have told us during training sessions that they have actually hung-up the phone since they were expecting a voice mail greeting. If in your mind, while the phone is ringing, you are expecting to hear a voice mail greeting and *if* you don't have your talking points ready then you will in fact be surprised when they answer the phone. The difference is that *you* have the talking points ready from Day 44. Frankly, all you have to do is use the same basic talking points you were planning to put into the voice mail message and go forward from there.

Prospect: This is Sally . . .

You: Good Morning, Sally, this is Bob Smith from ABC Company (pause to see if s/he makes a comment, asks a question and, if not, continue with the text below.

You: (Segue with something about the project or connection you found from your research). I understand from an article in the business journal that your company is growing and we just recently finished a project with a company similar to you and they were able to save close to 20 percent on their......(Pause to see if s/he makes a comment, if not continue with the dialogue below).

You: The purpose of my call today is to schedule just a brief appointment to understand a bit more about your (issue). I can share what we've done with others similar to you and then you can decide how or even if, you want to move forward.

You: (There are a number of different routes to go here, the easiest being to share a time when you will be near their physical location and offer an alternative). I'm going to be meeting with a client out by you next Wednesday the 23rd or I have some time the following week.

In most cases the prospect will ask questions or voice an objection. For today, make enough cold calls until you get a person to actually answer the phone and see how confident and prepared you are with your approach. And remember, your competition has given up a few calls ago so you are already in the lead!

Practice the talking points above prior to making your calls so you'll be even more prepared.

DAY 53
Objection!

Write down all the objections you have received in your selling career. If you are new to selling then ask some other salespeople at your company what objections you can expect to hear. Chances are that less than one (that's <1) new objection surfaces each year. If you are new to sales, most of the objections you hear have been heard by many salespeople before you. Frankly, it's shocking that most companies don't take the time to gather all the objections and develop talking points for each one before they send sales- people out into the fray of selling. Once you develop your talking points and practice them, out loud, and know them by heart your confidence will soar when making calls or handling objections face to face.

The logic for how best to respond to objections is based on three factors: 1) it's best to get the objection in the open and know what they are concerned about vs. them not raising the objection and leading you astray; 2) there is no objection that is new— every objection has been raised by at least one other prospect or customer; and 3) whatever you reinforce you get more of.

Here's how we recommend you develop your talking points for the objection responses. First, every objection is good to know (see factor 1). As a result, you want to reinforce the prospect/customer (see factor 3) so they will put on the table all their issues that might get in the way of doing business with you. Therefore, the first step we want to take is to reinforce that it's a good question or a good point. You do not always want to start with the same "that's a good question." Instead you will use other reinforcing statements such as "I'm glad you brought that up," "I see what you're saying," or "that's a good point." This approach will keep you from sounding defensive. If you do not understand with 100 percent clarity what they are objecting to it is essential that you immediately ask clarifying questions so you clearly understand the objection before you reinforce them and respond. When you ask a clarifying question you not only make certain your response will be on target but you also buy yourself time to determine the best response.

Second, you want to use one of the words "many, most, several or few" depending on how many of your existing *customers* initially had that objection and *still* decided to purchase from you or your company. So, for example, take the first objection you wrote down. Ask yourself the question, "How many of our existing customers raised this objection and ultimately ended up buying our product/service?" Is the answer "many, most, several or few"? For example, "I'm glad you brought that up, *several* of my customers made the same comment when I first started working with them…"

Finally, finish the sentence with the objection response. For example, "I'm glad you brought that up, *several* of my customers made the same comment when I first started working with them and they found that (specific objection response)." Make sure you answer honestly because the customer may want to know who these customers are and you need to be able to provide the answer.

Spend time today writing the talking points for each and every objection. If you "wing it" then you typically come off as flustered and desperate. If you write down the responses, practice them out loud, and commit them to memory you will respond in a confident and controlled manner. This will separate you from all the other competitors who are calling your prospect.

As the months and years pass you will come across a new objection every so often. When this happens make sure to develop talking points because it's sure to come up in the future and by having a well thought out answer you will be more confident!

Section 5: Appointments

DAY 54
Sales Octane Mantra #15—Bad News Does Not Get Better with Time

I have an aversion to delivering bad news in a timely manner. When I have bad news I tend to procrastinate as I try to figure out how to avoid dealing with the bad news. For some reason I think that it will get better and go away or that I will figure out a better way to deal with the bad news. Hence my statement, "Bad news does not get better with time." I've found that the sooner I make the call to deliver the "bad news" the less severe the response. The longer I wait the more severe the response. Basically it's a scientific calculation. The severity of the response is in direct proportion to the length of time it takes you to confront the "bad news." So, when (not if) you have an issue and have that nagging feeling that maybe it's better to wait, pick up the phone and deliver the news!

DAY 55
Sales Octane Mantra #16—Never Let the Facts Get In the Way of a Good Story. Note to Self: Facts Are Facts!

Several years ago a friend made the comment, "Never let the facts get in the way of a good story" in response to a discussion we just had where the facts did not line up. While this may be fine for story-telling it can become a problem for a salesperson who is not hitting their goals. Too often salespeople modify reality, their "story," in an effort to switch the focus from their shortcomings. Have you ever done this? If so you may feel better about the fact that you missed the mark but it does not change the fact that you missed the mark. You may modify the story so the finger points in a different direction but that does not change the fact that you missed the mark. Facts are facts. If you are not hitting your goals then the fact is. . .you missed. No amount of "spin" to your story will change this fact.

The way we explain our situation to ourselves and others has a major impact on how we will proceed in the future. If we constantly change the facts in an effort to shift the focus from our shortcomings then before long our brain begins to believe that what we are saying is true and we lose our desire to change, improve and achieve our goals. It's time to deal with the facts. You are now over 50 percent of the way through the Sales Continuum. Are you hitting your goals? If you are falling short of a goal then take accountability and deal with the fact that you need to make a change. It may be the goal you set is too high or it may be that you have not applied yourself. In either case something needs to change, and that's a fact. Once you begin to achieve your goals the "stories" take on a whole new light! You get the opportunity to share your wins, and achievements and that reinforces future effort. You get to discuss the obstacles you've overcome and these stories will reinforce your abilities. You're an achiever and that's a fact! For today take stock of the goals you've set for yourself and whether you are on track to achieve them. If not, you have two options. You can either modify the goal so it is attainable and make a commitment to reach the new goal, or you can apply yourself to the existing goal and overcome the challenges that have kept you from success. Don't change the facts of the story. Instead, go out and write a new story based on your achievement. You'll feel better about yourself and that's a fact!

DAY 56
Should I or Shouldn't I Confirm the Appointment?

By following the steps in the first fifty-five days you will get appointments with prospects. You have a few options relative to confirming these appointments. First, you can call the prospect a few days prior to the appointment and confirm that the appointment is still on their calendar. By confirming the appointment you open the door to a cancellation, however, one way to minimize cancellations is simply to call the prospect's office, and confirm with the administrative assistant or leave a message on their voice mail if there is no assistant. The following is an example of one approach:

"Good morning, this is Jim Ryerson from Sales Octane. I have an appointment with Robin tomorrow at 11 a.m. and I was just calling to confirm. Please tell her I'll see/call her at 11." Be presumptuous and to the point. You are a sales professional whose time is valuable and by confirming the appointment you send that message. Don't say something like "I want to make sure it's still on her calendar" as that's a sign of apprehension and plants the seed with the assistant that maybe they should drop everything and track down Robin or her calendar. This opens the door to a cancellation. By confirming you will be there you use the Law of Obligation that Robin will take the appointment when you arrive tomorrow. Remember, this is used when you've booked the appointment! (Don't use dishonest tactics like leaving this message and then showing up tomorrow at 11 when you did not initially have an appointment! See Day 42.)

The second approach is to pursue your prospect until you speak with them or their assistant and literally confirm that the appointment is on their calendar and they agree they still want to move forward. This will increase the possibility of them canceling the appointment simply because they have the opportunity to postpone/cancel right then and there. With the first option they have to take the time to call you back and postpone/cancel. This option may be appropriate when you have to travel a significant distance for the appointment with the prospect and/or if there are no other customers/prospects you could see in the area. The reason you would go to this extent to confirm the appointment is if you have a lot of business then you would rather know that the prospect is truly interested in your products/services as opposed to spending your time on a dead-end call.

The final approach is not to confirm the appointment and simply show up as scheduled. This is the path most salespeople take because they can learn something from physically being at the prospect's building or they have a product/service that lends itself to multiple departments and once they are in the building they can try to connect with contacts if their first appointment cancels.

The option you choose will change depending on your experience, your success and your schedule. Once you've shown up for several appointments and the prospect has cancelled (while you stand in the lobby) you may choose to confirm. Once you've become successful and your schedule dictates you confirm every appointment as a way of qualifying (if the prospect is willing to meet you that is a positive sign) you may pursue the prospect until you hear them confirm. In each case, show up on time!

DAY 57
Value Their Time and Yours

You send the message to the prospect you don't care about their business when you arrive late. You send the message that you are unprofessional when you arrive late. Your confidence will be shaken as you apologize and scramble to get your materials and thoughts together. Being on time sends the message you care about their business and that you are professional.

My experience is it takes 25 percent longer for me to get somewhere than what I initially thought. Issues with traffic, finding the correct address or finding the right office create anxiety and tension. Even phone appointments, if not planned properly, get off track when you can't find the number, or when you have the main number and getting a receptionist or dialing by name does not work. Our anxiety increases and our confidence drops. Leave early for appointments and dial early for phone appointments. My recommendation is to be five to ten minutes early for a face-to-face appointment. More than ten minutes and it may appear you have nothing to do. You will find that a few minutes of extra time are essential for preparing yourself and building your self-confidence while waiting for the prospect. By the way, if it is unavoidable (traffic, etc.) make sure to call the appointment and let them know your dilemma and the estimated time of arrival.

For today, take a moment and look at your calendar for the weeks ahead. Set time in your calendar to make sure you have adequate time to arrive on time! Make a commitment to being on time from this day forward.

DAY 58
You Never Get a Second Chance at a First Impression

First impressions matter and using reinforcing statements is a great way to start. When you reinforce someone, honestly and sincerely, they like you more. When you tell someone it's "great to meet you" you have reinforced them and they like you more. When your prospect achieves something, for instance if they just introduced a new product and it's getting positive press, and you say "I see your new product is doing very well" you have reinforced them and they like you more. This must be done *honestly and sincerely!* If you are doing this insincerely they will pick up on that and it will erode your relationship! During your research on Day 44 you should be looking for information that can be used to reinforce them early in your appointment or phone call. Even something as simple as commenting, "So, I understand that you are *in charge of* all the purchases of the organization" becomes a reinforcing statement because you have reinforced their position with the words "in charge of." They like you more! From the opening "It's great to meet you" to reinforcing their position or reinforcing an accomplishment you are building a positive feeling toward you and your organization. For today try making a few calls using reinforcement, *honestly and sincerely,* and see how the person responds. Pay close attention to their body language or their next statement over the phone after you make a reinforcing comment. You will see their positive reaction which will give you confidence and improve the probability of having a great call.

DAY 59
Walk and Talk Trumps Sit and Spew: The Face-to-Face Appointment

This step applies primarily to products or services that are used within the prospect's facility; however, several of the questions and techniques are applicable in all sales situations. After you greet your prospect and reinforce them, we recommend that you request a "walk-through" especially if your goods or services are used in their facility. The best way to position for the "walk-thru" is to make the statement/request "It would really be helpful if I/we could just take a quick walk through your space/facility/operation/plant." The word "helpful" gives them the indication that if they do the walk through you will be better positioned to bring value to their account. Second, it's not an open ended question like "Can we take a quick walk-thru" which has a 50 percent chance of getting the answer you don't want...NO."

There are two reasons why this will help. First, the prospect will be more comfortable walking and talking than they will be sitting across from you in an office or conference room. When your prospect is more comfortable they are more likely to share information. The second reason is you will learn more about them, their company, the opportunity, and you will be able to position yourself with other contacts in their organization. Here is what you learn about:

- The Prospect – You get to observe how they respond to others. Are they friendly with others, greeting and cajoling or are they all business as they walk? Do they provide a lot of detailed information and analysis about their business or are they less detailed? These observations will help you identify their behavioral style and how you should communicate with them.
- Their company – You get a good chance to pick up some visual indications of their company. We routinely assess attendees of our workshops to determine their learning style.

Are they visual – meaning they learn by seeing, are they auditory, meaning they learn by hearing or are they kinesthetic, meaning they learn by doing? The number of auditory salespeople was less than 2 percent. Visual was the top style and kinesthetic was the second most dominant style. Bottom line, most salespeople are visual learners, meaning they learn more by seeing than by simply sitting in a room talking and listening with the prospect. So, by walking around you get a chance to see the company, its culture and you'll position yourself for the third reason, to identify opportunities.

- The opportunity – When you walk around with them you play to your strength (visual) in terms of learning what type of opportunity you have. What products/services are they currently using, how is it working, what types of other products or services are they using? You may see a product or evidence of a service that is sold by a contact in your Wheel of the Fortunate lead group. This may be a good follow-up call to make for more information on your account strategy. You get a chance to see whether they buy on price or quality (low cost products/surroundings often mean low cost buyers while high quality products/surroundings often mean quality buyers).This is a great time to ask if it's okay if you take a photo of the current situation. Soften the request with a statement such as "it would really be helpful to my team if I had a photo of this, would it be okay if I took a picture?" In some cases the prospect will decline for security purposes. However, if they allow you to take some photos you win on three fronts. First, visual trumps written. When they say a picture is worth a thousand words they are correct. Even if you take great notes you will typically see more detail in a picture. Second, you get visual images you can use in your proposal presentation to reinforce the "pain" with their current situation. Your prospect is also most likely a visual learner. As a result, when you visually show the prospect their current situation during the proposal phase they will experience more of the pain and be more inclined to want to solve the pain. Third, after the sale you can take "after" photos so you now have "before and after" photos. This creates a very strong impact with future prospects.

- The "circles they run in" – There are a number of reasons you want to identify all the groups with which your prospect is involved. We refer to these as the "circles they run in." At the end of the Sales Continuum when the prospect has purchased from you and you are ready to ask for referrals (Day 95)it is essential that you have as much information as possible on the circles they run in. As you walk through their offices you should be looking for:

- Associations they belong to

- Boards they serve on

- Non-profits they are involved with

- Religious or fraternal organizations they frequent

- Sports groups they follow

- Academic institutions they support

- Industry or trade association memberships

- Community involvement
- Governmental

- And the list goes on

Keep your eyes and ears open for evidence of the circles they run in and not only will they enjoy your interest it will also position you for referrals after the sale!

- Other contacts - Finally you get a chance to meet other contacts within the account. Incidentally, since you are walking around with a "buyer" the presumption may be that you area key provider. Leverage that presumption by engaging others in a confident style. Don't just meekly smile at others, greet and engage them whenever possible.

Another question to ask during this early phase of the sales call is, "How long have you been with XYZ Company?" This provides you with a great deal of information that is essential to your sales strategy.

- New hire? – If they have only been with your prospect a short period of time then we know they are more willing to make changes. New hires have something to prove and are not typically committed to previous purchase decisions. So, if they use your competitor this is good news! If they use your product then your strategy must change.

- Involved with the previous purchase decision? – Once you know whose product or service the prospect is using *and you know how long your contact has been with the company* you can determine if they were involved with the decision to purchase the existing product. Remember, if they were involved in the decision then their natural inclination is to buy a similar product.

- Former employer opportunity? – If they have only been with your prospect a short period of time then you will want to ask "Where were you before you came here?" Their last employer may be a former client or you may know which competitive product they used. Also, since we now know this prospect recently left the other company this may represent another lead. If so, ask questions about their former employer. Employees are typically very open to sharing information about their former employer!

At your next appointment, after you greet them, make the statement, "It would really be helpful if I could just take a quick walk through your facility." Be prepared with the same questions you would normally use if they took you to their office only now ask them while you Walk and Talk vs. Sit and Spew!

DAY 60
First Things First: Preparing for the Call with the Driver and Influencer

We believe you can improve your sales results by identifying the prospect's behavioral style and the way they make buying decisions and then modify your approach at three points in the sales process:

- pre-call preparation
- the appointment/call itself
- follow up

Today we will cover how to prepare for a sales call for two of the four styles, Dominant/Drivers and Influencers and tomorrow we will cover Compliants and Steadies.

While many of the ideas we share today may already be part of your pre-call sales strategy we recommend aligning the steps with the customer's behavioral style.

Preparing for the Dominant/Driver

Here is how to prepare for a call with a prospect you have identified as having a Dominant/Driver behavioral style:

- What's in it for them $$$ – Because a customer with a Driver/Dominant behavioral style is bottom lined oriented we need to lay out the benefit(s) they will receive with our product/service early in the discussion. Be prepared to show how your product/service is a good investment and be prepared to get there *fast*.

- Develop a list of "best in class" references – Identify several "best in class" references that have used your product/service so you can share the list with them. Dominant/Drivers like to be associated with other "best in class" providers.

- Thicken your skin! – Dominant/Drivers tend to be direct, blunt and outspoken which may erode your self-confidence. Go into the presentation with strong self-confidence! (See Day 62)

- Stroke their ego – Driver/Dominants have a strong ego-drive and it would benefit you if you could share information that would reinforce their accomplishments. Do your homework and figure out where you could introduce these reinforcements into the sales call.

- They like to "own" the solution – Dominant/Drivers like to put their mark on decisions. Look for ways to tie their initiatives to your presentation.

- Have your facts! – Because the Dominant/Driver has a strong ego you should avoid disagreeing with them and instead focus on the facts. The key is to come prepared with the facts or you run the risk of disagreeing with them on a personal level.

- Develop an agenda – Driver/Dominants like structure and they are typically very busy. Bringing an agenda to the meeting gives them confidence you are not going to get off track.

Preparing for the Influencer

Here is how to prepare for a call with a prospect you have identified as having an Influencer behavioral style:

- Summarize your key points/handouts. Influencers tend to get off track and get you off track. As a result you need to have your key points summarized that go with your handouts or demonstration.

- Load up on the visuals. Influencers like to "experience" what they are buying and something that is visual has the greatest connection. Pictures, graphs, digital media, etc. Note: if your product/service is something that can be "trialed" this is another great way to connect with the kinesthetic learning style.

- Develop "cutting-edge" references for your product/service. Influencers love to be with the "in crowd" so sharing specific examples of who has used your product/service from that crowd will have a very positive impact.

- Bring a "compelling offer" along. If you have any special promotions or offers to act as an incentive this is important for Influencers who tend to be spontaneous. This "compelling offer" may just be the incentive they need to move forward.

- Remember the personal side. Take out your notes of what personal discussions you've had in the past. Or, if this is the first appointment, think of some personal prompts you may want to use during your first conversation. Influencers like to socialize!

For today take a look at the appointments (phone or face to face) you have with Drivers and Influencers and review the list. Prepare accordingly and you'll have more confidence going into the sale!

DAY 61
Sales Octane Mantra #17—It's a Level Playing Field, No One Is Better than You

You have a product or service your prospect will benefit from. You, or other salespeople from your organization have brought value to many customers in the past and you intend to bring value to your prospect. Why, then, do we feel inferior when we call on prospects? Why do we feel like we are at a disadvantage? They are no different than us. They may have come from a different area, been schooled at a different institution and followed a different career path but they have no more value than us. They may make more money and have more authority but they have no more value than us. That is, unless we choose to put them above us. Sales is a process that requires self-confidence and you determine how much confidence you take into each selling situation. Take a few minutes *right now* and list all the benefits you offer your prospect on a personal level. Let me give you a head start; are you friendly, positive, warm, empathetic, honest, cheerful, kind, sensitive, pleasant, considerate, passionate, energetic or thoughtful? Now take a few minutes *right now* and list all the benefits you offer with your product or service. What value will they receive with your product or service? How will they feel when they have your product or service? By the time you are finished with this brief exercise you should have a full page of positive results you offer your prospect on a personal and business level. This list should increase your self-confidence! Take a look at it *every day* for the balance of this book and you'll recognize that *no one* is better than you! Make your sales calls
with confidence!

DAY 62
Sales Octane Mantra #18—You Are What You See and Visualization is the Key!

When you think of yourself in a selling situation what do you see? Do you see yourself confident and knowledgeable? Do you see your customers trusting what you say and genuinely liking you? Do you see yourself bringing real value and solving real problems? Do you see yourself exhibiting passion for your product and/or service? Visualization is a key technique used by sales professionals and is one of the many ways that sales professionals differentiate themselves from the rest of the pack. Professional baseball players visualize making solid contact between the ball and bat. They don't visualize missing. Professional golfers visualize the flight path of a perfect shot as the ball lands in the ideal location. They don't visualize going into the water. Why is it that many salespeople do not take advantage of this powerful tool called visualization? In my experience it's because they feel it's arrogant to presuppose they will be successful. They may feel this would only make a failed event more difficult. "Prepare for the worst and you'll seldom be disappointed" is their motto. The motto of the sales professional is "You are what you see and visualization is the key!" Take your list from yesterday and develop word pictures in your mind as to how you look when you display each of the personal characteristics on our list. Literally project this image in your mind. Then take the list of benefits your customers will receive with your product and develop word pictures of how they will respond when they experience those benefits. Keep this list with you, review it several times a day and before sales appointments!

You are what you see and visualization is the key!

DAY 63
First Things First: Preparing for the Call with the Compliant and Steady

While many of the ideas we share today may already be part of your pre-call sales strategy, we recommend aligning the steps with the customer's behavioral style.

Preparing for the Compliant

Here is how to prepare for a call with a prospect you have identified as having a Compliant behavioral style:

- Have all the information – Compliants ask a lot of questions and will become suspicious if you do not have the answers. It's best to be over-prepared versus under-prepared with a Compliant! This information might include:

  1. pro's and con's of each option you are offering
  2. financial parameters & justification for each option
  3. any reputable third-party industry information about the options

- Be honest – If you have a situation that has not worked with your product and the prospect may know about it then be prepared with an answer should it come up!

- Develop a list of credible references – The key word is credible. If there's anyone who will actually follow up on your references it will be the Compliant. Also, if you have a credible reference that would be willing to speak with the Compliant (it is best if the reference *also* has a compliant behavioral style) compile that information before the call.

- Handouts with data – If you have handouts that have additional data this may be helpful to dispel their suspicion or help you answer questions. Oftentimes the Compliant will ask a question the salesperson cannot answer and then the Compliant will find the answer for the salesperson in the handouts!

- Develop a list of internal advocates within the company (if this is a multi-department sale) – If there is someone within the company that has successfully used your product/service you may even decide to have them participate in the sales call.

- Develop your presentation in a step-by-step approach making sure to cover all the information you believe they would ever need.

- Develop an agenda – Compliants like structure and bringing an agenda to the meeting gives them confidence you are not going to get off track.

As you can tell from the length of the list, calling on Compliants requires additional preparation. Build this into your schedule if you typically call on prospects with a Compliant behavioral style.

Preparing for the Steady

Here is how to prepare for a call with a prospect you have identified as having a Steady behavioral style:

- Remember the personal side – Take out your notes of what personal discussions you've had in the past. Or, if this is the first appointment, think of some personal prompts you may want to use during your first conversation. Those with a Steady behavioral style like people and enjoy a light personal conversion!
- Go lite with the details – Have top-line information prepared for your presentation, like a headline in a newspaper, since the Steady style is not as much into the details. Have the backup information in case they have additional questions.

- Show me! – Develop evidence of how your product/service has worked and also other solutions on the market that have not worked. The Steady wants to make sure they are not the first to try your product/service.

- Develop a list of credible references – Also, if you have a credible reference that would be willing to speak with the Steady (it is best if the reference *also* has a Steady behavioral style) compile that information before the call.

- Be honest – If you have a situation that has not worked with your product and the prospect may know about it then be prepared with an answer should it come up!

- Bring a "compelling offer" along – If you have any special promotions or offers to act as an incentive this is important for a Steady who tends to be resistant to moving quickly. This "compelling offer" may just be the incentive they need to move forward.

For today take a look at the appointments (phone or face-to-face) you have with those of a Compliant or Steady behavioral style and review the list. Prepare accordingly and you'll have more confidence going into the sale!

DAY 64
Take Notes and Use Forms

If you've ever had professional landscaping done on your home you've inevitably experienced the reason why we are passionate at Sales Octane about taking notes. Here's the scenario. Landscaper A arrives and tours your yard as you tell them what you are hoping to accomplish. You tell them specific details such as wanting to protect a particular planting or shrub that is important to your spouse. You explain your vision of what you are looking for, the problems with drainage you want to correct and the list goes on. All the while Landscaper A is nodding, agreeing and even engaging with you, but they are not taking a lot of notes, if any. You begin to suspect that they may not be getting everything you are saying, or worse, that what you are saying must not be as important to them as it is to you! After they leave you begin to wonder whether your spouse's plantings will be history and the drainage problem will be addressed! This makes you very uncomfortable with Landscaper A.

Now let's take a look at the alternative. Landscaper B arrives and asks, "Would it be okay if I took some notes?" This calls attention to the fact that whatever you are going to be saying must be important to them otherwise why would they ask if it was okay to take notes? As you give Landscaper B specific details such as wanting to protect a particular planting or shrub that is important to your spouse they confirm you with "Ok, that's important so we want to make sure that we keep these plantings and shrubs right where they are in the final plan." You explain your vision of what you are looking for and again they confirm it with "Just so I make sure I have it, you said you wanted to etc, etc., is that right?" And when you mention the lack of drainage that you want them to correct they even clarify with questions like "So, what kind of problems does that cause?" and "How long has it been this way?" Your confidence soars as you believe Landscaper B has a grasp of what you are looking for by confirming what you said you needed. You are more comfortable that you will get what you want as this person wrote down what you wanted! Sales professionals take notes and they use forms with prepared questions to help remind them of what is important!

For today, take your questions from your qualification exercise on Day 31. Add those to your appointment/call form to make sure you properly qualify every sales situation, from an incoming call to a major appointment. Next, if your company has a "customer evaluation" form with specific questions regarding your product or service incorporate that form with your qualifying questions. If you do not have a "customer evaluation" form then use the qualification questions to begin the process and you add additional questions as they surface in future chapters. Go ahead, take a few minutes today and type up the questions into one concise form you can use when you are making calls.

Note: If you primarily work with a computer program/contact management software to gather your notes then make sure to develop the fields for each of the answers so you are prompted to ask the questions!

DAY 65
Get Ahead on the Call! Confirm The Timing, Agenda and Situation

Before forging ahead with your sales presentation we recommend always confirming the timing, agenda and situation. This is critical if you are on a subsequent sales call or an appointment where you are presenting a proposal with pricing, details, drawings, and so forth. We will cover a subsequent appointment tomorrow. For today, we want you to understand the steps and get comfortable with the process.

First, by confirming the timing of the appointment (ten minutes, one hour, two hours, etc.) you minimize their anxiety about how long this will take. This can be as simple as "As I mentioned last week this should only be thirty minutes..." This puts them at ease and they become more receptive to what you are going to say.

Second, by confirming the agenda you show the prospect you are prepared and that you have a plan for the appointment. If your prospect has a Driven or Compliant behavioral style you will want to have an actual written agenda that you present to them or send them via e-mail before the call. This can be as simple as "I plan to ask you some questions about...and then share our new product... and give you some preliminary numbers."

Third, after sharing the agenda it is optional to confirm with the prospect that if this will meet their needs then you expect them to move forward. You can create a subtle obligation by positioning that *if you can find something that might work for them* that *perhaps they would be willing to take the next step.* Even a small obligation by the prospect at this early stage puts you in a better position when it's time to close. This can be as simple as "If we can find something that addresses your situation and will give you what you are looking for then does that sound like something that might work for you?" Even if they give you a qualified answer such as "Sure, if the price is right" or "Yes, but I will be looking at other providers before I make a decision," you have learned some very important information that you can craft into your sales call. You can ask them, "What price point are you looking for?" or "Who, other than our company, are you going to be looking at?" In either case you have tried to get them to make an obligation and that will make a difference later in your sales call.

Finally, you will make a statement about their situation *as you understand it* and then confirm if you have it correct or if anything has changed. Regardless of what you are selling, when you finally have an appointment over the phone or face to face there is a reason they have agreed to meet with you and there is a reason you have pursued them. By confirming *that reason or situation* (which should be easy if you've done your homework) you create a great start to the sales call. For example, let's say you sell software and the reason you are meeting with the prospect is to share how your software might be a good choice with their productivity initiatives.

This step would sound similar to this, "Thanks for the opportunity to meet with you today. As I mentioned last week this should only be thirty minutes. I have an agenda here. . .as you can see I plan to ask you some questions about (the particular product/service you are selling) and then share some details about our new software and answer any questions you may have. If we can find something today that meets your needs my goal is that you'd be willing to use our solution. Will that work?" "It's my understanding that you are looking to move on this soon, is that right?"

That's it! You've clearly covered the timing to put them at ease, you've covered the agenda and even expressed your expectation for them to move forward which may have created obligation on their part and you've started with a confirmation of the situation *as you know it.*

As your appointment nears the time allocated, you want to be the person who acknowledges you are almost out of time. For instance, let's say the appointment was at ten in the morning and you asked for twenty minutes. As you near the twenty-minute mark it is essential that you interject, "I see that our time is almost up?" Or, if you still have some critical information you have not yet shared (hopefully because you've done a great job with questions and your prospect has been speaking most of the appointment) you would interject, "I see that our time is almost up and there are a number of points I've not yet shared." In either case, you've reinforced to the prospect that you value your and their time. If the prospect has been speaking for most of the appointment they are usually quick to offer their apologies and suggest that they have more time. This will reinforce that you have done a great job and they are interested! If they have another commitment and you've done a good job on the call they will typically ask to reschedule for another meeting. Again, this will reinforce that you have done a great job. Depending on the situation you can offer to come back again or extend the existing appointment. If, however, you have not connected with the prospect then it's better to know sooner rather than later (See Day 55).

For today take your product/service and write out your opening statements for either a phone-to-phone or face-to-face sales call. Even though your sales situations may vary tremendously it is essential that you write out the typical language so it is embedded in your mind. Also, you should say it out loud several times once you have written it. If it does not sound good when you say it out loud then it will not sound good in front of the prospect. Take the time to find the right words that work for you and your prospects will see the difference! This will also increase your confidence on sales calls.

Do it now, don't wait!

DAY 66
Don't Spill Your Marbles on a
Subsequent Call!

Yesterday you developed your opening for a sales call. Today we want to take a few minutes and cover the opening of a subsequent sales call, more specifically the subsequent sales call where you are prepared to share your proposal, pricing or details with the prospect. There is nothing worse when new information surfaces such as a change to the schedule or the criteria *and you find out after you've reviewed your proposal with the prospect.* When they say, "Ok, this looks good, but we were talking the other day and decided we wanted to change this..." your proposal is now going to have to change. If your price changes, prospects may become suspicious and you will have to back pedal in an effort to regain their trust. This step is meant to surface any changes to the prospect's situation *before* you provide pricing or details.

On subsequent calls you will follow the same steps as Day 66. You will thank them for the opportunity to get back together again, share the timing, review the agenda and then confirm the situation as you left it the last time. Only this time you will finish with "Has anything changed?" It's essential that you ask the question "Has anything changed?" before you spill your marbles! If it's a subsequent appointment *and* the situation has changed it's best for you to know this new twist at the beginning versus after you've shared your proposal. This will allow you to make a mid-course correction and respond to their new situation. For example, suppose you are on a subsequent call where you will present the proposal with pricing and details. You confirm the timing, the agenda, the situation and then you ask "Has anything changed?" Now, what if they respond that things have changed? What if they say the schedule has slipped and it's going to result in a delay of several weeks or months? This may have an impact on how you want to proceed. Do you want to share your detailed proposal and pricing knowing that it will be sitting around for a long time before a decision might be made? When proposals sit around the competition always seems to get a look and that may put you at a disadvantage.

Even if the prospect wants to see your proposal with the details you can make a decision whether you want to leave anything with them. A good response is, "There's a good chance your needs may change given this delay so let's walk through the proposal I have with me today and then if you'd like I will send you a preliminary proposal with budget numbers. Then, as it gets closer and you have your final needs established I can firm up the quote."

If they say the schedule is still the same but they have been looking at some other options, which they like, and *you* now have some new competition? This allows you early in this sales call to determine how much information you wish to share or how you might approach the proposal you have in your briefcase! In this situation you can say, "Based on what you've told me today I would like to go back and work with our team and provide an alternative proposal."

In most cases the situation does not change. In most cases the prospect will respond to your question, "Has anything changed?" with "No, that's where we're at." That affirmative statement will give you increased confidence as you begin to share your proposal.

For today ask someone to role-play a prospect who says, "Yes, we have made some changes" and "Yes, we've been looking at a competitor who came in with another product that we like." You need to get comfortable as you transition from this new and disappointing information into your next step.

DAY 67
Who's Doing All the Talking? Great Questions Equal Great Commissions!

Now that you have started the sales call properly the next step is to uncover the "What?" the "Why?" and the "How?" "What is the prospect looking for, Why are they looking for it and How will they make the decision? When you launch into your sales presentation the prospect feels like they are being sold and you learn absolutely nothing about their situation. *You* learn very little when *you* are talking. Bottom line: everyone loses. At the point the prospect believes you have what they need then you have taken the first step towards helping them buy from you.

Question #1 "What are you currently using?"

This very simple question helps you identify the following things:

- What they currently use will give you an indication of what you are up against. In most cases you know the competition and can begin to develop your strategy based on this single piece of information.

- In many cases what they currently use and whom they get it from go together. If you are not sure, ask the follow-up question, "Whom did you get it from?"

- What they currently use is a good indication of what they will use in the future. If they purchase high quality today and your product is also high quality that is a good sign. If they purchase low quality (price buyer) and you are the feature rich solution. . . it's best to know sooner rather than later. Situations can change so you may want to ask a follow-up question during your sales call to confirm who chose the current product/service with a question such as "Who made the decision to purchase this product?" If the prospect you are currently talking to participated in the decision to purchase the low quality solution then you want to go to the next question. If, however, the prospect you are currently talking to was not part of the decision then this may put you in a better position. Knowledge is power and knowing what they have and who bought it is powerful information.

- The prospect's willingness to share information and the detail they provide to this question will give you a good indication of how the prospect is likely to communicate throughout the sales process. You can pick up additional insight into their behavioral style as you listen to their responses.

Question #2 How is it/that working for you" and/or "What do you like about it?"

This simple question helps you identify the following things:

- Whatever a prospect likes about their current product/service they are seldom willing to give up on their next purchase. If you have power windows and you like them you are most likely not going to go back to a hand-crank window. Whatever features you like in your current product/service is the baseline for what you will have to provide to get in the game.

- You will get insight into how the prospect values certain characteristics of your product/service. Are the things they share with you about the image, function or quantifiable results? Are they talking glowingly about the provider versus the product?

- Depending on the number of things they share you may get insight into how satisfied they are with the product/service. If they keep talking about all the things they like about their current product or provider it may seem like bad news for you. However, we know that it is best to get this out on the table sooner rather than later.

- In many cases when the prospect says what they like about their current product/service these may also be characteristics of *your* product *or, better yet,* you may have even greater features, advantages and benefits than their current supplier. *Don't* interrupt them or start selling! That will appear defensive, desperate and pushy! Instead, take good notes which you can use later.

Question #3 "What, if anything, are you trying to improve?"

Note: the question *is not* "What don't you like about your current product/service?" That negative approach makes it way too obvious that you are looking for dirt on the competitor so you can sell against them. When you ask what they would like to *improve* you are using a positive pairing (see Day 34). Also, your request to identify things they want to improve is not specific to the product or the service. You're not going to ask "What, if anything, with the product/service you have today are you trying to improve?" You are asking "What, if anything, are you trying to improve this time around?" In some cases they will bring up larger issues, some of which may not be directly related to what you are selling. You want them to think broader than their current situation and dream of ways to *improve* their current situation. Finally, by using the modifier of "if anything" reinforces that we are not suggesting that the existing product is not meeting their needs. We are simply asking what, if anything, they might be trying to improve! This simple question helps you identify the following things:

- Areas of discontent. If they do not like something about their current product/service you may get them to share it with you as a result of this subtle question. Don't jump on these issues, just take notes!

- Desired Features, Advantages or Benefits. The prospect may share specific features they have heard about and would like. They may share some of the advantages they would experience if they were able to find a particular feature. They may even be willing to share how that advantage would specifically benefit them.

- Big picture issues. In some cases the prospect may begin to share larger initiatives and paint a picture of what would be a dream situation.

DAY 68
Ask Them How They Are Going To Buy from You?

Question #4

The final question is, "Walk me through your decision making process; how are you going to make this decision?" You are trying to uncover both the steps they will take to make this decision and also who, other than themselves, will be involved. This simple question helps you identify the following things:

- Their knowledge/authority. Their answer will tell you a lot about their knowledge of the situation and their authority. If they offer a lot of detail they are most likely knowledgeable about and have authority with this purchase. If they offer little or no information they are probably not the final authority or the final person you need to speak with about the situation.

- Who else is involved? You may learn about other departments and people involved with the decision. One follow-up question can be, "Who, other than yourself, will be involved in this decision?" This question gives them the positive reinforcement that you believe they are involved and opens up the question to identify other key decision makers.

- Criteria/Specifications. Often they will share the specific characteristics of the product/service they desire if they've not already done so. Occasionally they will use vague references such as, ". . .and then we'll decide what we're looking for, and then look at several options. . . " In this case, you earn the right to ask a clarifying question such as "When you say, we'll decide what we're looking for, what specifically *are you looking for?* This short follow-up question keeps them talking and allows you to learn!

- Timeline. As they share information, keep track of the steps. When they are finished you can review and then ask, "Given these steps, when do you expect to make the decision?" Note: The prospect seldom, if ever, has a detailed plan for their decision making process so be prepared for awkward silence. Don't interrupt! The prospect is piecing together their decision making process in their mind and they often voice their answers as they piece it together.

For today tailor the questions to your particular product or service. If you have a particular product or service that involves a distribution channel such as a distributor, broker, representative or retail outlet then you may have more questions. For instance, you may ask, "What are you currently using?" and also, "And who are you purchasing it from?" You may ask, "How is that working for you?" and also, "And how is that distributor working out?" Finally, you may ask, "What, if anything, are you looking to improve this time around?" and also, "What, if anything, are you looking to improve from a distribution standpoint?"

Handling their questions

It's inevitable that during the appointment the prospect will ask several questions about your product, service and company. It's important to clearly understand their question before you respond. Similar to handling objections on Day 53 you want to reinforce them when they ask a question since whatever you reinforce you get more of. When they ask a question the first step you want to take is to reinforce that it's a good question or a good point. You do not always want to start with the same "That's a good question." Instead you will use other reinforcing statements such as "I'm glad you brought that up," "I see what you're saying," or "That's a good point." This approach will keep you from sounding defensive and it will invite additional questions. If you do not understand with 100 percent clarity what they are asking, it is essential that you immediately ask clarifying questions. When you ask a clarifying question you not only make certain your response will be on target but you also buy yourself time to determine the best response. Once you write out the questions practice them out-loud until you are asking them in a very comfortable confident style!

DAY 69
Sales Octane Mantra #19—Plan Your Work and Work Your Plan

I heard this statement many years ago and it is a great concept that bears repeating. C. Northcote Parkinson once wrote that "work expands to fill the time available for its completion." It's often referred to as Parkinson's Law. If you think about Parkinson's Law it is absolutely true. If you are working on something, for instance developing a proposal, then the time it takes you to complete the proposal often expands to fill whatever time you have available to complete the task. If you have two hours and it's reasonable to complete the proposal in two hours, then you'll most likely finish the task in two hours. However, if you start in the morning and you have the entire day available you will probably take the better part of the day to complete the proposal simply because you have that much time available.

Think about how much work you accomplish several days before you go on vacation. You're totally focused. You don't take on anything that is not essential because the time available to complete the task at hand is limited by when you leave on vacation. What if you were to work like you were going on vacation at the close of every day! Would you be tempted to engage in nonessential activities and discussion (complaining around the water cooler for instance)? Would you be tempted to respond to those e-mails that could wait until tomorrow if they need to be addressed at all? C. Northcote Parkinson was right. By planning our work and working our plan we will increase our productivity and grow our sales volume. Make your plan at the end of the day for the following day. Map it out so you have intermediate deadlines throughout the day. Stay on task and see how much you accomplish!

DAY 70
Sales Octane Mantra #20—First and Fast Do Not Always Go Together

Sales professionals are human. We want to see progress. In many cases that means we are tempted to do things first that we can get done fast so we feel like we made progress. Items like organizing our desk, returning a call from a friend or checking our e-mail are typically "fast" items that we jump at because the completion of the task will feel like progress. At the same time we tend to avoid activities or issues that are difficult or challenging like making a call on an open proposal (fear of confrontation), developing a list of target accounts (fear of commitment) or making prospecting calls (fear of rejection). The idea that just because you can do it fast means you should do it first often backfires when we surface new issues while organizing our desk, get into a long complicated discussion with our friend or get caught up in responding to multiple e-mails that take much longer than we initially expected. At the same time, we eat up precious time with these "fast" activities that could be devoted to more important commitments we've made such as meeting our sales goal, following up on open proposals, developing a list of target accounts, making prospecting calls. Remember, just because you are going to do it first does not mean it's going to be fast and just because you think it's going to be fast does not mean you should do it first.

Stay on task!

DAY 71
Silence Is Golden. Keep Your Prospect Talking!

Several years ago one of our daughters was working through a word scramble where you take a word and change the order of the letters to spell another word. That particular day one of the words was *listen*. Take a few seconds and try to figure out what other words you can make from the word *listen*. Okay, you may have come up with Enlist or you may have come up with what our daughter found that day...the word silent. I remember thinking how ironic it was that the best strategy to improve our ability to listen is to remain silent and they both share the exact same letters! Silence is golden. Unfortunately, the motto of many salespeople is "selling is telling." They cannot wait to tell people about their product or service. The minute they get an audience over the phone or face to face they begin telling their story. They feel that if they spew enough information something will connect with the prospect. Hopefully you feel comfortable asking the questions we discussed on Day 66. Those questions will get the prospect talking and hopefully uncover key information that you can leverage as you continue the appointment.

What we want to share today is the importance of using follow-up questions that keep the prospect talking so you can make sure you have *all* the information before you share your sales presentation.

When you ask a prospect any of the questions we've developed to this point they will give you an answer and you typically respond in one of four ways:

1. They will give you an answer which leads beautifully into a sales pitch for a particular feature, advantage or benefit associated with your product or service. In this case you will

launch into how your product/service will solve that issue. Huge mistake.

2. They will give you an answer that you're 90 percent sure you understand and you will go on to the next question. Huge mistake.

3. They will give you an answer that you do, in *fact*, understand completely and you will go to the next question. Huge mistake.

4. They will give you an answer and you will follow the process we're about to share with you. Brilliant choice!

Throughout the entire questioning process it is extremely important you do not offer a lot of solutions or advice as it will confirm to the prospect you are only interested in selling them something as soon as possible. This will make them uncomfortable and cause them to resist even if they need your product/service.

If they respond with an answer which leads beautifully into a sales pitch for a particular feature or advantage of your product or service write it down and keep going. It's acceptable to offer an occasional confirmation that you have seen a similar situation in the past or that you helped someone with a similar situation in the past. But these confirmations should be infrequent and certainly not every time the prospect shares a need with you.

If you are not 100 percent sure you understand what they have shared it is important to clarify. Something as simple as, "When you say ___ you mean?" This will often get them to share additional information. Also, you can simply repeat the word they just said and make it a question. For instance, a prospect says they are looking for more timely delivery. Simply ask "Timely delivery meaning?" In either case the prospect will share additional information.

Even when you know exactly what they mean you should prompt them to share additional information. The first question, "What are you currently using?"/"Who are you buying it from?" is usually fast. You may need to ask if they are the sole supplier or are there other products they are purchasing. Or you may want to ask how long they have been using that product/service or supplier.

Once you ask the second question, "How is that/are they working for you?"/"What do you like about it/them?" do not go to the third question until you are sure they have exhausted their answers to the second one. We have found that there is typically more than one answer for the second and third questions and, most importantly, the first answer is seldom their most important issue. It's almost like they have to "warm up" to the question with a few easy answers before they get to their most important issues. The way you keep them going is by prompting them with "What else?", "Anything else?", "Is that it?" or "Is there anything else you can think of?" This will take some practice. We are typically busy writing notes of what they are saying and then once we finish writing the notes, the prospect has finished talking and we feel pressured to launch into our sales presentation or go to the next question. It will take practice to feel comfortable asking "Okay, what else?" Another technique is that while you are taking notes or once they have finished their answer you simply repeat the end of the answer and then ask "What else?" For example, if they mention timely delivery, you respond with, "Okay, timely delivery, what else?"

Only use the question, "Is that about it?" when they have given several responses to the second or third question and you feel like they have exhausted their answers. The goal of this process is to make the prospect comfortable with you, get more information that will be helpful in developing your strategy and finally to keep you from talking!

Practice asking these questions with a prospect today! Add them to your "questionnaire" from Day 64.

DAY 72
Raising the Temperature: The Pain-Reliever Approach

Now that you have the prospect talking, there are a number of different questioning techniques to keep them providing information. Our goal is always to uncover their needs, wants and desires expressed as "pain." Here's what I mean.

A sterile approach to the transaction known as "selling"

Whatever the prospect needs, wants, or desires has a cost which we, the salesperson, refer to as the investment required to obtaining our product or service. At the same time the prospect is evaluating whether the investment is a good value in terms of meeting their needs, wants or desires. The key is for you, the salesperson, to show value equal to or in excess of what the prospect feels the need, want or desire is worth. In many cases you also have to show that the value of your product or service exceeds that of other options (competitors, different direction, etc) the prospect might be considering. In order for you to understand the "value" the prospect will place on solving the need, want or desire you have to understand the cost of not fulfilling the need, want or desire. We refer to that cost as "pain." Unmet needs, unmet wants, and unmet desires are painful. The more "pain" the prospect associates with the unmet need, want or desire the more they are willing to invest. In some cases the prospect may not even know they have a need, want or desire and you have to help them see the pain they must resolve. So, your job is to become the Pain Reliever.

In a typical call the prospect states a need, want or desire often expressed as a problem. The salesperson then runs immediately to the solution they can offer. This may continue with a few stated problems and the salesperson immediately answers with their solution. Eventually the prospect gets to the price question, there's a negotiation and finally you win the sale or the prospect goes down one of several alternative paths:

1. the prospect turns to another competitor who has made their case as a better value

2. the prospect decides not to purchase at this time because they failed to see the value in solving their problem

3. the prospect no longer has the ability to buy (no money)

While this process often works there are a number of problems. First, even if you win the fact that you did not raise the pain with good questioning skills means you have left money on the table. Second, if *you* did not raise the pain with good questioning skills and your competitor did (even if their product/service was inferior to yours) they may have been able to convince the prospect that their product/service was a better value. Third, if *you* did not raise the pain with good questioning skills the prospect may not have recognized the importance of resolving the pain and therefore decided to forego the purchase. You lose and the prospect loses.

By asking more questions to uncover pain you improve the probability of closing more sales, at a higher price, eliminating competition and helping more prospects experience the value offered with your product or service. Everyone wins.

We refer to this as the Pain Reliever approach. There are several reasons why this approach works:

1. It makes your prospect more comfortable with you. When a prospect mentions a need, want or desire (typically expressed as a problem) and you immediately jump to how your product can solve the problem you minimize the importance of their problem. The prospect may have had this problem for some time and they've not been able to resolve the issue. Along you come and tell them you have just what they need. This may raise suspicion and suspicion is not what you want the prospect to feel. Also, by asking more probing questions you become a consultant who is there to help them diagnose

their pain. This creates confidence in your ability and the prospect becomes more comfortable with you!

2. You learn more about their needs, wants, and desires because they are talking. With each passing minute the probability increases that you will uncover a new pain or an additional need, want or desire because they continue to talk. Every additional issue you uncover increases the value you bring which further justifies your product or service.

3. They begin to buy. With each issue that surfaces you have the opportunity to confirm with them whether this is something they want to resolve. This question may be as simple as, "So, is this something that *if* we could find a solution would help you avoid...?" If they respond in the affirmative, "Yes. That would help me. . . " then they have begun to obligate themselves to you. It is very subtle but powerful. They begin to buy with each small obligation! This only happens if you are uncovering pain and discussing the results that occur with the pain and the value of resolving the pain.

4. You're not talking. Yes, the final reason this approach works is that it keeps the customer talking and you silent. When you're silent you listen and when you listen you learn.

For today observe how you respond to the initial questions of your prospects and/or customers in a sales situation. Do you answer every question in terms of exactly what you can do or do you ask questions to identify the pain associated with the needs, wants, desires or "problems" they raise?

DAY 73
The Reverse & "Columbo" Questions: Raising Additional Issues

The Reverse

The easiest of the questioning techniques to uncover pain is the reverse. Our three daughters were masters of this technique when they were younger. They would come to me on a Saturday afternoon and ask me a question such as, "Dad, can you bring me to the movies?" Inevitably I would be working in the yard or engaged in another activity that I could not meet their spontaneous (and untimely) request. However, my response of, "No, I'm sorry honey. I can't right now" was seldom met with an empathetic "Okay, Dad, thanks anyway." Instead I would get the usual "Why not?" to which I would add some detail such as "I'm working in the yard right now and I need to finish this." Seldom, if ever, did *that* end the questioning. They would continue to ask and I would continue to offer more information. Here's the learning: with each subsequent "Why?" or "Why not?" or "Why do you have to do it now?" or "Why can't you just take me and then finish?" my daughter would ask, I would *offer additional information, insight or clarification.* I would never simply respond "I'm working in the yard right now and I need to finish this" like a robot. Our desire to provide more information is a conditioned human response. The good news is you can plan on this conditioned human response and make it work for you in your effort to uncover a prospect's pain. There are a number of very simple responses to the prospect's initial and subsequent statements that will influence them to give you *additional information, insight or clarification.*

Here is a partial list of these simple "reverse" responses you can use:

- How so?

- Really?

- Meaning...?

- Why is that?

- How big of a problem is this/that?

- Why do you think that is?

- How long has this been an issue?

- How often does this/that happen?

- And when that happens. ..?

- And...?

- When you say _____ you mean?

The struggle you may have with this process is that many salespeople want to be liked or want to appear knowledgeable, both worthy goals. However, expressed another way it sounds a bit different: many salespeople have a fear of being disliked or fear of appearing unknowledgeable. As a result they want to answer every question so they appear knowledgeable and the prospect will like them more! The opposite actually happens. By being the "know it all" they routinely suggest solutions that are not on target because they did not clarify what the prospect was really looking for. The prospect begins to think the salesperson does not listen or does not understand their situation. The salesperson is doing most of the talking and the prospect begins to feel like they are being sold. The very thing the salesperson wanted to avoid, being seen as unknowledgeable and not being liked, is exactly what they get!

The Columbo Approach

The "Columbo" approach is a bit more difficult for exactly the same reasons we just mentioned. When I was growing up there was a show called "Columbo." The bumbling detective often appeared confused and would frustrate his suspects by asking obvious questions. While our goal is not to frustrate our prospects, the technique he used is effective when combined with the reverse technique. Here's how it works. When the prospect mentions a need, want or desire that fits perfectly with a feature, advantage or benefit of your product/service you may want to use this approach. Instead of responding "I know what you're talking about, that problem must cost you a lot, the good news is our product/service is proven to improve this issue!" try the following:

"So, what I hear you saying is that problem is costing you a lot...I, mean. . .how big of a problem *is* *that*?" Much like the reverse, the fact that you asked a question that appeared to have already been answered will illicit additional information. Our hope is that the additional information will add clarity to the pain and possibly even surface additional concerns or pain. Also, because you did not immediately jump on the problem with your solution you appear less concerned with getting a sale and more concerned with understanding all the issues associated with the initial problem (helping them buy!).

Slow down and use these techniques. For today, write the list of reverse questions, even the simple one or two word reverse questions, on your notepad before you make your phone or face-to-face calls. Routinely use reverse questions and get more information. Occasionally use a "Columbo" approach so the reverse questions. Do not appear too programmed. The
"Columbo" will slow it down!

DAY 74
The Neutral Response and Negative Reverse Questioning Techniques

The Neutral Response

Occasionally prospects will raise a number of concerns about your product or service that are not really objections but rather statements to keep you on edge. General statements such as "Price will be important" or "Make sure you sharpen your pencil" are a common refrain that tend to put us on edge. Often the prospect will mention a competitor's strength, possibly a particular feature, benefit or advantage that is unique to them. Here are a few examples: "You know, XYZ competitor claims they can ship in six weeks!" (and you're at ten weeks); "Your competitor says they will underbid the lowest price of any manufacturer!;" "Your competitor has a local presence here in (not where you are located);" "XYZ competitor is one of the largest providers in the area." Our tendency as a salesperson is to address every single detail the prospect raises, sort of a back and forth game of ping-pong. At times this immediate response to each statement appears as if we are defensive. We may even appear agitated as every response we give brings yet another concern or statement about the competitor or the prospect's desire to keep the cost down. If you catch yourself with a prospect that has an endless supply of concerns they wish to share and you suspect they are just trying to keep you on edge you may want to use the Neutral Response. As the name suggests, you will go into "Neutral" and simply not respond with a rebuttal nor challenge their statement. Statements like "Price will be important" or "Make sure you sharpen your pencil" can be met with the Neutral Response of "I understand, price is an important consideration...". By not reacting with a series of additional questions about what they mean or responding with how you are the most cost-effective solution you simply "neutralize" the statement with "I understand, price is an important consideration." You will frequently catch them off guard and they will go onto another subject.

- "You know, XYZ competitor claims they can ship in six weeks!" (and you're at ten weeks) can be "neutralized" with "Lead time is an important issue."

- "Your competitor says they will underbid the lowest price of any manufacturer!" can be "neutralized" with "Price is an important consideration."

- "Your competitor has a local presence here in (City)" can be "neutralized" with "Having a local presence is certainly a consideration."

Try to identify the concerns or issues your prospects have mentioned over the past seventy-three days that seem to be an effort on their part to keep you on edge. Write these statements down and decide on the best Neutral Response to use. Once you've written them and said them out loud several times you will be able to recall them whenever you meet a prospect that raises these types of issues or concerns.

Negative Reverse

The Negative Reverse goes along with the Neutral Response technique; however, the Negative Reverse is only used as a last resort. If the Neutral Response does not end the continued string of issues or concerns then you may want to use the Negative Reverse. Let's set the stage. The prospect is qualified; nonetheless, they continue to raise concern after concern. They may even suggest that their current situation could not be any better. Depending on how you obtained the appointment there are two approaches. If the prospect agreed to meet with you and then continues raising concern after concern the Negative Reverse would go something like this "Bob, based on what I'm hearing you say. . .why *did* you even agree to *meet with me?*"

If you are on a cold call and the prospect continues to raise concerns or questions about even considering another option the Negative Reverse would go something like this "John, based on what you're saying, why did you even agree to take my call and meet with me?" If you're saying to yourself this sounds like a risky approach you're correct. However, if the prospect is truly satisfied and is so confident of their current situation then you are probably wasting your time. As you will see on Day 90 when you say "No" to something you say "yes" to something else. Saying "no" to this prospect, frees you up to say yes to better prospects!

Occasionally by using the Negative Reverse the prospect may back down and give you the reason they agreed to meet with you or take your call. While they may not immediately warm up to you at least you now have an opportunity to decide if the reason why they took your call or met with you justifies your continued investment of time.

Each minute of your time is precious. Don't waste additional time unnecessarily with a prospect whose questions suggest they are trying to put you on edge or that they'd be foolish even considering your solution. Use the Neutral Response and if that does not turn the conversation then try the Negative Reverse. You won't lose because there's probably nothing there to lose!

Take a few minutes to write out the Negative Reverse response and say it out loud until you own the statement. Now you're prepared for the worst case scenario!

Note: Many of the behavioral characteristics and adaptations noted in this section of the book are taken from work done by Target Training International. © 2005-2013 Target Training International.

DAY 75
Adapting to the Dominant/Driver on the Call

People buy from people they like. This is not news to anyone. Prospects are more comfortable buying from a sales professional they like but they also are more comfortable, and willing to purchase, from a salesperson similar to them. And while similarities in age, background, nationality, lifestyle and even dress are shown to create a positive response our focus is on behavioral similarities. If you recall back on Day 8 we discussed the importance of modifying your approach to mirror, in a very subtle way, the style of your prospect. Issues such as rate of speech and volume of speech are two obvious examples. We now want to take this concept a step further and discuss *specific* ways in which you need to adapt during the sales call, whether on the phone or face to face, depending on the behavioral style of the prospect. The type of adaptation you make will also depend on your style. Take your dominant behavioral style(s) from Days 2 and 3. Today we will cover the adaptations you should consider making when you identify your prospect has a Dominant/Driver behavioral style (from Day 4).

If your behavioral style is also a Dominant/Driver then consider adapting in the following manner:

- Present your information in a linear, organized manner. Go step by step and be prepared to speed up as they direct.
- Be direct. Get to the point quickly as they are typically impatient.

- Move fast as they are comfortable deciding quickly.

- Offer alternatives during the conversation. Allow them to decide between options as they want to make the decision.

- Give them recognition. Use "you said/wanted/asked, so I" types of comments to reinforce their ego.

- Look for opportunities to let them win. They enjoy a challenge and winning is important. Make sure that you also achieve your goals!

- Disagree with the facts, not the person. It's okay to stand firm, however, disagree with the facts and not with them on a personal level.

- Don't dictate to them as being in control makes them more comfortable with you.

- You also like a challenge so enjoy the combat! They expect you to hold your ground.

- It's a two way street. Don't let them overpower you.

If your behavioral style is Influencing/Social then consider adapting to the Dominant/Driver in the following manner:

- Avoid physical contact. Actions such as putting your hands on their back and touching their arm are off limits. Drivers like their space and this includes their personal space (attention close talkers).

- Do not joke. Your natural desire to create levity will be unappreciated.

- Be direct. Get to the point quickly as they are typically impatient.

- Avoid getting off-track. Present your information in a linear, organized manner. Go step by step and be prepared to speedup as they direct.

- "Stay in form" with business. Don't become too personal in the discussion. They typically focus on the business outcome. Follow their lead relative to any personal discussion.

- Look for opportunities to let them win. They enjoy a challenge and winning is important. Make sure that you also achieve your goals! Give them recognition. Use "you said/wanted/asked, so I..."types of comments to reinforce their ego.

- Avoid ambiguity or uncertainty. They reward knowledge and confidence.

- Take copious notes. This reinforces that what they are saying is important.

- Do not over-promise. Your natural desire to please the prospect may cause you to over-commit. Avoid this trap at all cost.

- Confidently close. Your natural desire to avoid confrontation may deter you from moving the sale forward. Ask for their business.

- Don't let them overpower you. You have a goal so don't allow them to overpower you.

If your behavioral style is Steady/Amiable then consider adapting to the Dominant/Driver in the following manner:

- Strengthen your resolve. Mirror the strength of the Driver since they will typically be strong. It's okay to remain friendly but strong.

- Take copious notes. This reinforces that what they are saying is important.

- Be confident! Don't let them intimidate you. You have a go also don't allow them to intimidate you.

- Present your information in a linear, organized manner. Go step by step and be prepared to speed up as they direct.

- Speed it up! You must proceed faster than you feel comfortable during the call. Drivers move fast!

- Give them recognition. Use "you said/wanted/asked, so I..."types of comments to reinforce their ego.

- Look for opportunities to let them win. They enjoy a challenge and winning is important.

- Avoid ambiguity or uncertainty. They reward knowledge and confidence.

- Disagree with the facts, not the person. Stay focused on the facts and details when not in agreement.

- Close sooner! Your natural desire to avoid confrontation may deter you from moving the sale forward. The Driver appreciates the value of moving the sale forward so ask the question.

- Don't let them overpower you. You have a goal and you must achieve that goal so don't allow them to overpower you.

If your behavioral style is Compliant/Analytical then consider adapting to the Dominant/Driven in the following manner:

- Be brief and to the point. Get to the point quickly as they are typically impatient and direct.

- Touch upon the high points. The Driver is interested in the bottom line.

- Do not over-use data. Your natural tendency is to cover all the data. Touch upon the high points and only share the additional data *if* the Driver requests it.

- Speed it up! You must proceed faster than you feel comfortable during the call. Drivers move fast!

- Give them recognition. Use "you said/wanted/asked, so I..." types of comments to reinforce their ego.

- Satisfy their strong ego. Look for opportunities to reinforce them and their accomplishments.

- Look for opportunities to let them win. They enjoy a challenge and winning is important but make sure you also achieve your goals.

Put this information into a format where you can easily access it as you prepare your call strategy with a prospect/customer.

DAY 76
Sales Octane Mantra #21—When You Pursue a Working Knowledge Of Sales You Are Pursuing Success. Sales Is Your Craft!

The average manager reads **less than two** books per year on the topic of management. While that number is staggeringly low, I imagine that it is even lower for most salespeople. Salespeople tend to read about their products or services but few invest in a working knowledge of the sales discipline. Sales is your craft! Much like law is the craft of those in the law profession and medicine is the craft of those in the medical profession. These two occupations are the highest paid occupations in the world. It makes sense since they invest heavily in continuing their working knowledge of their craft. They never think they've arrived! Look at these high earners and apply the same skill so you can earn as much as they earn. Read books and magazines on the subject of sales, listen to audio books, seminars and speeches on the topic of sales. Attend seminars and web-based programs on the topic of sales. Join sales associations both within your industry and local sales association chapters. Develop relationships with other sales professionals and spend timesharing and refining your ideas and techniques around selling. Set a goal for how many books (audio/hardcopy) you will review or read, seminars, speeches or webinars you will attend, associations and sales networks you will join. Plan the work and work the plan! This is your craft! Invest in your sales knowledge!

DAY 77
Sales Octane Mantra #22—Hard Work: This Process Known as the Sales Continuum Is Hard Work!

You are now over three quarters of the way through the Sales Continuum process and you have no doubt realized how much work is involved. There are connections to make, calls to make, questions and responses to objections to learn, techniques to assimilate, research to complete, organizations to join, materials to read and it takes a while before the hard work pays off. How long you ask? It depends if you follow the steps in this book and *stay with it* regardless of the hours and the amount of effort required. When I say *stay with it* I mean literally without interruption. We used to take our children to a park near our home. Along with all the state of the art playground equipment there was a deep rut around the merry-go-round from the adults who dug their feet into the ground to get the merry-go-round moving. It was hard work to get the merry-go-round started. However, once you got it going you could stand back and occasionally push one of the bars of the merry-go-round as it went by. Frankly, it would continue on its own for some time, slowing down but not at a noticeable rate. Eventually the merry-go-round would slow down if there was no additional effort to keep it going.

The Sales Continuum process is much like that merry-go-round. It takes a lot of effort and hard work to get started. Once it's going it requires less effort to maintain. If, however, you stop with any of the steps in the process you will begin to lose momentum. This traditionally happens once you start to grow your sales and you get involved with the minutia of performing.

Over time your opportunities, sales volume and income will drop off. Getting it back up to speed at that point takes just as much effort as you put in at the start! However, if you work hard at all the steps in the Sales Continuum, even when you begin to have success, you will be thankful you stayed with it!

DAY 78
Adapting to the Social/Influencer on the Call

Today we will cover the adaptations you should consider making when you identify your prospect has a Social/Influencer behavioral style (from Day 4).

If your behavioral style is Dominant/Driver then consider adapting to the Social/Influencer in the following manner:

- Be personal and friendly. Warm up the appointment with a sincere conversation around something personal.

- Don't be in a hurry. Take your time. The appointment may not stay on track so don't appear in a hurry as that will make the buyer uncomfortable.

- Joke around. Have some fun. Follow their lead.

- Allow them to talk. They love to talk so don't dominate.

- Provide recognition. They enjoy being reinforced so look for an opportunity to provide recognition.

- Don't talk down to them. Your natural tendency to lead the conversation may be interpreted as talking down to them. Be careful!

- Talk about people. They enjoy talking about others and their experiences so look for opportunities to leverage similar contacts and interests.

- Prepare for a lot of spontaneity. The conversation may appear to be unstructured with spontaneous thoughts and "off the track" discussions. Allow them the flexibility to get off track and they will be more comfortable with you.

- Keep the presentation at a high level. Don't get mired down in details as they will lose interest.

- Share ways to minimize risk and get them into the product/service sooner! As they see the risk go down, they will move forward.

If your behavioral style is also Influencing/Social then consider adapting to the Social/Influencer in the following manner:

- Be yourself. Have fun on the call and generate energy from their stories.

- Let them talk more than you. They should be doing most of the talking as they are more comfortable when they are talking.

- Listen to their stories. They enjoy sharing stories so don't interrupt or attempt to "one-up" them.

- Give them the recognition. Look for opportunities to give them recognition during your presentation.

- Look for opportunities to weave in your product/service presentation. Be careful not to waste too much time talking about your product/service. They will view this as "business" and may be uncomfortable.

- Make sure you achieve your goal. Your tendency to enjoy the conversation must be balanced with your need to achieve your goal.

If your behavioral style is Steady/Amiable then consider adapting to the Social/Influencer in the following manner:

- Minimize the details. Keep the details to a minimum as you share with them the benefits of your product/service.

- Listen to their stories. They enjoy sharing stories so sit back and enjoy the conversation.

- Have fun with them. Enjoy the discussion!

- Allow them to talk but make sure you keep the call on track.

- Give them recognition. Look for opportunities to give them recognition during your presentation.

- Share ways to minimize risk and get them into the product/service sooner! Make it easy for them to accept your product/service.

- Share key dates and problems. Share with them any time sensitive deadlines and confirm the problems that surface throughout the call. Use these deadlines to move the call forward.

- Make sure you achieve your goal. Keep a clear line of sight to your goal during the call as their lack of focus may distract you.

If your behavioral style is Compliant/Analytical then consider adapting to the Social/Influencer in the following manner:

- Keep the presentation at a high level. Don't get mired down in details as they will lose interest.

- Use the summary information whenever possible. Minimize your natural approach of covering all the details by offering summary information.

- Prepare for a lot of spontaneity. The conversation may appear to be unstructured with spontaneous thoughts and "off the track" discussions. Allow them the flexibility to get off track.

- Be friendly and fun. Leave your detail focus behind and instead think about being more friendly and fun on this call.

- Ask more questions. Instead of stating information turn it around. Look for opportunities to link their answers to your goal.

- Allow them to talk but make sure you keep the call on track. Let them do most of the talking but steer the conversation towards your goal.

- Share ways to minimize risk and get them into the product/service sooner! Make it easy for them by reducing their risk.

Put this information into a format where you can easily access it as you prepare your call strategy with a prospect or customer.

DAY 79
Adapting to the Steady/Amiable on the Call

Today we will cover the adaptations you should consider making when you identify your prospect has a Steady/Amiable behavioral style (from Day 4).

If your behavioral style is Dominant/Driver then consider adapting to the Steady/Amiable in the following manner:

- Don't control or dominate. Methodically go through your presentation and allow them to decide how fast they wish to proceed.

- Personal first. Begin with your personal connections to build rapport.

- Show sincerity. Be honest and sincere during your presentation as they are very good at sizing up character.

- Start with the problem/issue and move slowly through each option and confirm there are no questions following each one: "Does that make sense?" or "Did I cover that okay?"

- Listen carefully. Pay attention to the conversation and don't appear to lose interest. This makes them less comfortable with you.

- Slow down. Your natural approach is to move directly and quickly through the agenda. This will make them very uncomfortable. Slow down and relax.

- Build trust. The steady is typically suspicious and you must move them to a point where they trust you.

- Give them the facts they need. Don't go too deep with information; stay on a higher level with less detail.

- Tie everything you can back to what they currently use or are comfortable using. They do not like to change so tie your product/service back to what they are comfortable using.

- Get "little" agreements along the way. Ask confirmation questions such as "Is this what you're looking for?" or "Does this look like it will work?" They are very loyal buyers so getting them to agree along the way begins to obligate them.

- Do not push. Take your time. They will not proceed fast; however, they are very loyal buyers so the longer sales cycle is worth the investment of time.

If your behavioral style is Influencing/Social then consider adapting to the Steady/Amiable in the following manner:

- Be friendly, personal and earn their trust. Lower your energy level a bit and use your natural personality to build a friendly, personal environment.

- Let them talk. You ask questions. Your natural tendency is to share information rapidly. In this case you want to ask more questions and let them talk!

- Slow down. Your natural approach is to talk fast and have a lot of energy. This will make them very uncomfortable. Slowdown and relax.
- Start with the problem/issue and move slowly through each option and confirm there are no questions following each one: "Does that make sense?" or "Did I cover that okay?"

- Give them the facts. Don't "wing it" with details. Share factual information that you can stand behind.

- Provide assurances of your promises. Share references or guarantees to minimize their risk. If this is a change from their current situation these assurances are essential.

- Get "little" agreements along the way. Ask confirmation questions such as "Is this what you're looking for?" or "Does this look like it will work?" They are very loyal buyers so by getting them to agree along the way will begin to obligate them.

- Tie your solution back to what they currently use or are comfortable using. Whereas you may like to change and make spontaneous decisions they do not like to change so tie your product/service back to what they are comfortable using.

- Do not push. Take your time. They will not proceed fast; however, they are very loyal buyers so the longer sales cycle is worth the investment of time.

If your behavioral style is also Steady/Amiable then consider adapting to the Steady/Amiable in the following manner:

- Be yourself. Move through the call in a very relaxed and comfortable manner and lean toward a friendly discussion.

- Provide assurances of your promises. Share references or guarantees to minimize their risk. If this is a change from their current situation these assurances are essential.

- Be factual. Give them the facts of your offering but don't go too deep with information; stay on a higher level with less detail.

- Assure them. When they agree with a particular point you should assure them they are headed in the right direction.

- Expand your "team." Introduce them to or mention your managers, service managers and other team members to increase their confidence with your team.

- Tie everything you can back to what they currently use or are comfortable using. Identify the ease of going with your product/service.

- Keep sight of your goal. Make sure you accomplish your goal!

If your behavioral style is Compliant/Analytical then consider adapting to the Steady/Amiable in the following manner:

- Make it personal. Begin the call with something personal. Avoid launching into the details of the call too quickly.

- Move slowly. Set aside ample time for the call as it will move more slowly than sales calls with other behavioral styles.

- Provide facts and figures. Have the detailed facts and figures but keep the conversation at a higher level. You can go into greater detail if they ask for more detailed information.

- Do not over control or push. Your natural tendency to control the details and push through the extensive information you brought may cause the buyer to disengage from the conversation.

- Develop trust by providing assurances. Share credible references and guarantees that will build their trust in your product/service.

- Tie everything you can back to what they currently use or are comfortable using. Identify the ease of going with your product/service.

- Focus on reliability and service. Share information regarding the reliability of your product and service to satisfy their risk-averse nature.

Put this information into a format where you can easily access it as you prepare your call strategy with a prospect/customer.

DAY 80
Adapting to the
Analytical/Compliant on the Call

Today we will cover the adaptations you should consider making when you identify your prospect has an Analytical/Compliant behavioral style (from Day 4).

If your behavioral style is Dominant/Driver then consider adapting to the Analytical/Compliant in the following manner:

- Be patient and slow. Don't allow your Driven nature to make them uncomfortable.

- Give them data! Make sure you bring all the detailed information that supports your presentation.

- Use handouts with data. The more material you can share with them the more credible your case.

- Give more information than you'd like. Go above and beyond what you would normally expect a customer would need to make a decision.

- Start with the issue and move slowly through each option and confirm there are no questions following each one; "Does that make sense?" or "Did I cover that okay?" Be detailed.

- Give them credit. Reinforce them sincerely and honestly throughout the call by giving them credit for their questions and/or concerns that support your product/service.

- Keep control. Your driven nature may cause you to get frustrated with their cautious approach so be aware of your persistence.

- Keep it all business. Do not talk personally unless they initiate a personal discussion. Even then, keep it to a minimum and get back to business.

- Do not push. They make thoughtful, careful decisions and will become suspicious if you continue to push them toward a close.

- There will be many questions coming your way so don't get defensive. If you don't have the answer, identify how you will get the information and confirm they are comfortable with your plan/timeframe.

- Stress the "reality" of the risk associated with not moving forward (if they consistently show an inability to move forward).Be careful not to raise "unrealistic" risks or you will lose credibility fast.

If your behavioral style is Influencing/Social then consider adapting to the Analytical/Compliant in the following manner:

- Keep your distance. Respect their space and do not touch if you are on a face-to-face call.

- Do not be too personal. Cordial is one thing but your natural social style will make them suspicious. Keep it friendly but direct.

- Give them the facts, figures and proof. Give them more details than you would be comfortable receiving if you were in the buyer's position. They want details so give it to them.
- Do not waste time. They will want to stick to business so respect their desire and stick to the agenda.

- There will be many questions coming your way so don't get defensive. If you don't have the answer, identify how you will get the information and confirm they are comfortable with your plan/timeframe.

- Start with the issue and move slowly through each option and confirm there are no questions following each one; "Does that make sense?" or "Did I cover that okay?" Be detailed.

- Answer all their questions. Don't dismiss any of their questions. If they ask it then you must answer it.

- Reference the source of any information you share that is not your own. Your credibility is one of the pieces to the puzzle of connecting with this style. Make sure you share the sources of your information in an effort to gain credibility.

- Be concerned with details. Take an interest in their detail orientation. Even if you don't feel it is important to the decision, if they are interested you need to be interested.

- Confirm you have given them what they want along the way. Continually check in with questions like "Is that what you were looking for?" or "Is there anything else you need on that point?"

- Occasionally reinforce them sincerely and honestly by giving them credit for their questions and/or concerns. Being accurate is important to them so reinforce that characteristic.

- Stress the "reality" of the risk associated with not moving forward (if they consistently show an inability to move forward).Be careful not to raise "unrealistic" risks or you will lose credibility fast.

- Don't be surprised if it takes more than one or two meetings. Don't spill all your marbles with the first call.

If your behavioral style is Steady/Amiable then consider adapting to the Analytical/Compliant in the following manner:

- Keep your distance. Respect their space and do not touch if you are on a face-to-face call.

- Do not be too personal. It's okay to be friendly and cordial but avoid trying to be their friend. Instead be direct and follow their lead regarding personal discussion.

- Do not fear their skeptical nature. Do not take their skepticism as a lack of confidence in your sales ability. This is their nature so recognize their constant questioning as a desire to make a correct decision.

- Start with the issue and move slowly through each option and confirm there are no questions following each one: "Does that make sense?" or "Did I cover that okay?" Be detailed.

- Follow through on details. Go deeper in the details than you would normally go if you were making a similar decision.

- Occasionally reinforce them by giving them credit for their questions and/or concerns. They pride themselves on making good observations so reinforce this characteristic.

- Answer all questions with facts. Avoid offering your insight or personal input and stay focused on the facts. Their decision will be made with factual information so give them everything you have in your bag.

- Reference the source of any information you share that is not your own. Credibility is an essential characteristic to help them become more comfortable with you and your product or service so provide your credible source(s) of information.

- Stress the "reality" of the risk associated with not moving forward (if they consistently show an inability to move forward).Be careful not to raise "unrealistic" risks or you will lose credibility fast.

- Don't be surprised if it takes more than one or two meetings. Don't spill all your marbles with the first call.

If your behavioral style is also Compliant/Analytical then consider adapting to the Analytical/Compliant in the following manner:

- Be yourself. Your natural tendency to stay focused on the task at hand will connect with the buyer and make them comfortable with your approach.

- Give them the data they request. Provide them with the detailed answers they are looking for *even if you would do it differently.*

- Examine pro's and con's. You will naturally evaluate your own product or service before you proceed with selling it to a prospective buyer. Share the pro's and con's you used with your evaluation as this will make them confident in your analytical abilities.

- Remain in control. Your natural desire to be accurate may cause you to engage should the buyer choose a different path. Remain in control and allow the buyer to choose their own path.

- Provide evidence. Provide credible references and evidence to support your claims.
- Stay focused on your goal. Your natural approach is to focus more on the process of making the decision and less on the outcome. As a sales professional you must balance your desire to help the buyer make a correct decision with the need to meet your goal of a sale! Don't lose sight of that goal.

Put this information into a format where you can easily access it as you prepare your call strategy with a prospect/customer.

DAY 81
"Have I got it?" Letter of Understanding: Creating Obligation

Near the end of the initial call you should have determined the next step. We recommend you tell your prospect you will be sending them a document (e-mail, written correspondence, etc.) confirming the discussion points just to make sure you "got it."

Go back to your office and type up your notes from the call and organize them in the following order: Current Situation, Results/Challenges and Next Step(s).

Step 1. The Current Situation

The Current Situation is all of the basic information they may have given you about their project, company and what is driving this project/inquiry. For instance, let's say they shared with you the size of their business, the number of employees they have, the current products they are using, some of the issues they are experiencing with the current product and their needs, wants or desires relative to this situation.

This confirms you listened and took an interest in what they were saying.

Step 2. Results/Challenges

The Results/Challenges include any of the results, pain or problems they are experiencing as a result of their current situation.[1] For instance, if they shared with you that the situation with their current supplier is that the shipments are frequently late, that's the current situation[1] – it does not speak to the pain or results of that issue. Because you probed during the sales call you may have found out that the late shipments cause the production line to shut down and the shutdown causes lead time issues which cause customer complaints.

Write down these details in the document under the heading of Results/Challenges. This now reminds the prospect that the issues they shared result in real costs, real pain and are real problems that need to be addressed. The fact that you have taken the time to summarize them will reinforce to the prospect that you are organized, focused and a real sales professional.

Step 3. The Next Step(s)

Now write the next steps you spoke about at the end of the sales call under the heading of "Next Steps." This may include additional work on their part or yours. Perhaps you agreed to get them additional information, some budget numbers, or they agreed to get you some specifications or additional information.

Creating Obligation

At the end of your "next steps section" you will write a simple obligation statement. The obligation statement is meant to confirm with the prospect that when you do something they will do something. This may seem presumptuous but this step is absolutely necessary. It's not as if you are writing "If I send you this budget figure you agree to buy everything from me." It could be something as simple as "Once you receive my information you will evaluate it with your team and if our product/service meets your expectations you plan to move forward and award the order by August 1."

On the surface this simple statement is just confirming what they told you. It's subtle and a bit presumptuous; however, they are likely to take the entire document as a whole (The Situation, The Results/Challenges and The Next Steps) and respond with either a "Yes, you got it" (meaning99 plus percent of the Situation, Results/Challenges and Next Steps are correct) or "No, you missed my point" (because something major was missing or incorrect from your Situation, Implications or Next Steps). Rarely will they single out the obligation statement.

You will typically receive one of three responses:

Response #1 – "You got it."

When you receive this response your confidence will increase. The prospect has just reinforced that you correctly identified the Situation, Results/Challenges and Next Step. Incidentally, they have also obligated themselves in a very minor way.

Response #2 – "You got it but after you left I had another thought" or "You got it but after you left I spoke to another team member and they had a different idea."

When you receive this response, your confidence will increase. This type of additional communication and clarification confirms they are interested. They read your e-mail/document, thought about it and even shared your information with others. Chances are your competitors do not have this additional information!

Response #3 – "This looks good to me but I want to have some others take a look to make sure I've covered everything."

When you receive this response your confidence will increase. This response will typically lead to other contacts within the account. These other contacts may believe the company is already working with you since your name is on the material. This improves your position within the account. They are definitely interested if they are sharing your information around the company!

Seldom, if ever, will you receive a negative response to a "Have I got it?" letter of understanding. Build the obligation and watch how the prospect consistently follows the obligation! For today, take your most recent appointment, draft the "Have I got it?" letter of understanding and put it in an e-mail or letter to the prospect today! Learning this discipline will reinforce your need to take comprehensive and accurate notes and use the questioning techniques we covered earlier in the book. You are beginning to wrap all the details together of the Sales Continuum process into a tight, comprehensive sales strategy.

DAY 82
Following Up for the Next Step:
Don't Delay, Call Today!

One of the common questions I get from sales people is how often they should follow up with a prospect and the frequency of those calls. The second question is "When do I give up?" These questions apply to both initial Prospecting calls and following up after an appointment in an effort to get to the next step. Very few of your initial calls will result in a return call from a prospect. It's not because you are doing a poor job with what you are saying on your calls. It's not because they don't want your product or service. It's because they are busy and you are one of many who are trying to get their attention. Your persistence and disciplined follow up will pay off. So, the short answer to the question "When do you give up?" is not for a long time!

The issue of frequency depends on a number of issues:

1. Your product/service. In some cases the sale is time sensitive so the frequency of your calls will increase.

2. A deadline. In some cases you may have a project related product/service so there are immediate deadlines when the prospect will select vendors and the frequency of your calls will increase as the deadline nears.

3. Your forecast. If you really need the sale you are more inclined to select a more frequent call cycle.

4. The "next opportunity" – Once an opportunity to sell passes (they select another provider) you may want to stretch your frequency to once a quarter or even longer depending on your industry.

At no time during your follow-up process do you want to give the prospect the impression you are desperate. If you constantly call them with the same exact message, it appears you are desperate.

There are several key follow-up techniques that will improve the probability of making that connection sooner rather than later, regardless of the frequency.

In most every case you want to leverage the first technique, *I'm a busy sales professional approach.*

"I'm a busy sales professional" Approach

The intent of this approach is to help the prospect see how busy you are with other projects, customers and appointments. You want them to have the impression that other customers are buying from you! If they believe other customers are buying from you they are more inclined to think about buying from you. Psychologists call this Social Influence. For example: (voice mail, e-mail, snail mail).

"I'm going to be tied up/working with a project/customer, appointment for the next couple of days so I'll give you a call on Thursday, or, if there's a better time feel free to call me on my cell phone/phone at 1-800-IAM-GOOD that's 1-800-IAM-GOOD. Thanks and have a great day."

"Deadline" Approach

If you honestly and sincerely have a deadline that might encourage them to return your call, include that in your message. For example:

"There's a price increase that goes into effect the first of the year...if you were able to order before the 31st..."

"After I returned to the office" Approach

If you have additional information that was not shared during the last appointment/call then offer that in your message as follows:

"I was running through some new information on our product/service and found something I think might help in your decision..."

"As you requested" Approach

If there was something the prospect requested during the call and you agreed to follow up then remind them of that fact in your message. For example:

"As you requested, I've sent the information in the mail on the XYZ...I'd like to schedule a brief phone conversation for next Friday, the 22nd to understand the next step...I'm going to be out of town..."

"I have one more question" Approach

Many times you will think of other questions you want to ask the prospect after the initial call. You may leave the question with your message; however, that minimizes your opportunity to connect with face to face or phone to phone with the prospect. For example:

"I went back and pulled together the pricing information you requested and ran across a couple of questions...I'm going to be out the office with customers..."

"Another customer, similar to you, just went with us and I wanted to share with you" Approach

If, since your last contact, another customer decided to invest in your product or service then this becomes a useful strategy to get a return call. By sharing with the prospect that another customer has decided to use your product/service you again leverage the concept of Social Influence. For example:

"I found out another customer, XYZ, just went with us and I wanted to share with you how they are using the product/service."

"I promised" Approach

Last but not least is the "I promised" approach. We are attempting to create an obligation with the prospect by reinforcing that we have done what we said we would do. This statement can be used at the start of any message *when you've told them you would call on a specific day* in either a previous message or a previous meeting/call. For example:

"As promised, I'm calling back to see if you have any questions on the information we discussed... I'm going to be with clients most of tomorrow..."

Always remain in control of the next step

You never want to accept "I'll give you a call in a few days/weeks/when we have a decision." from a prospect. You are now at the mercy of the prospect. Even if they ultimately do call you back and give you the order, the intervening days pass like years as you wait for the call. Instead, whenever they say "I'll give you a call in a few days/weeks/when we have a decision" clarify as to what day, what week or approximately when they anticipate having a decision. Then, whatever they respond with you should check your schedule and confirm that you "have a commitment that day" so *if* you don't hear from them by noon (that day) you will give them a call. Now you're in control! For example:

Prospect: I'll give you a call as soon as we have a decision.

You: "Great, when do you think that will be?"

Prospect: About a week

You: (Looking at your calendar) "You're thinking April 20? I've got a full calendar that day so if we don't connect before noon I'll give you a call in the afternoon."

That's it; you now have the ball in your court.

Often the prospect gets so busy with other issues that even if they are planning to go with you they forget to call you on that appointed day. Instead of you wondering why they have not called and fearing the worst *you are in control* and you will make the call. The prospect will see you as busy, organized and conscientious.

In many cases you will combine two of the approaches together in an attempt to obligate the prospect to a return call and leverage the principle of Social Influence that other customers are buying your product or service. Practice several of these today with your follow up calls and *don't give up.*

DAY 83
Sales Octane Mantra #23—It's Not About Being Right, It's About Getting What You Want

Many times your prospects and customers will be wrong (you know it happens...and you may jump to correct them). Many times the people who support your sales efforts from your own company will be wrong (and you really want to correct them). In both situations you may want to set the record straight and be *right!* Get over it! It's not about being right; it's about getting what you want. This is not in any way a recommendation to be devious, mischievous, selfish or manipulative. Integrity is at the core of our approach. Before you move forward and correct your prospect/customer ask yourself this question. "Is being right going to help me get what I want?" If the answer is "no," then don't bring it up. In many cases "setting the record straight and being right" will erode your position and decrease the probability you will get what you want. Set your ego aside and ask yourself "Is being right going to help me get what I want?" whenever you feel the urge to "set the record straight?" You will be seen as a great person whom people will like and want to buy from.

DAY 84
Sales Octane Mantra #24—
Discipline: Inspect What You
Expect, What Gets Measured Gets
Done

On a recent flight I spoke with the CEO of a corporation with 1,200 salespeople. When I told him what I did and the title of this book he passionately stated that his company could tell within 90 days whether someone would make it as a salesperson. I believe him! Within the first few months your activity will reveal whether you have the self-discipline to become a sales professional. The salespeople who set goals, develop measurements to confirm how they are progressing against those goals and then do whatever it takes to meet those goals have the self-discipline to become a sales professional. They earn far more than their counterparts, they grow their business faster and they are in greater demand in the marketplace! The good news is you can learn to have self-discipline; it's not something you are granted at birth. While you can learn to have discipline the key indicator will be your ability to set expectations and meet or exceed those expectations. And while this is something that will continue for your entire selling career it is critical in the early stages to constantly measure and inspect how you are doing compared to your goals. Inspect what you expect because what gets measured gets done…by the sales professional!

DAY 85
How to Follow Up Properly Based
On the Buyer's Behavioral Style

There are specific follow up steps to use based on the behavioral style of your prospect you identified on Day 4.

Dominant/Driver follow-up

1. Follow up as promised. Drivers are very results-oriented and keep their commitments. They expect others to do the same and keep their commitments. Whatever you commit to doing for a Driver make sure you meet or exceed that commitment in the timeframe promised.

2. Give them credit. When you follow up with a Driver it's a good strategy to give them credit for anything they pointed out or clarified during or since the call.

3. Manage the expectations. Be detailed with what they should expect from you along with specific timeframes.

4. Continue to mention credible references. Drivers are egocentric and like to be associated with other important individuals. Reference anyone they may find impressive in your correspondence.

5. Nurture with knowledge. Drivers like to be in the know so constantly send information they may find useful. This keeps your name in front of them while providing them with valuable information.

6. Expand your reach. Sometimes the Driver is so focused on another result that they put your issue on hold. If you are not getting a response, evaluate working with others who are significant to your contact.

Influencer/Social follow-up

1. Follow up often. Influencers tend to over-commit which means they may have other new issues that put your issue out of sight and mind. By following up often you increase the probability they will re-engage with you.

2. Put something in that is personal. Come up with something personal to include with your follow-up. Whatever their interest (sports, family, stock market, etc.) they will be more inclined to connect with you if it's not all business.

3. Follow up with the "rest of the information." If you did not give them the detailed information as a "take-away" from your appointment this makes a great reason to follow up. Get the detailed information in their hands fast especially if there are others involved in the decision making process (who are Drivers, Steadies or Compliants)

4. Use a "take-away." If appropriate, reinforce what they might miss if they wait too long. This may be just the push they need to get them over the edge and return your call!

Steady/Amiable follow-up

1. Come up with something personal to include with your follow-up. Whatever their interest (sports, family, stock market, etc.) they will be more inclined to connect with you if it's not all business.

2. Don't push. Maintain a reasonable follow-up process with a little pressure, especially if they have told you they have a pressing date/issue. They are very patient and expect others to act in a similar patient manner.

3. Create a tipping point. Making them aware of an upcoming price increase, change in the product line or lead time extension are reasons that might get them to return your call. However, do not pressure them as that will backfire!

4. Limited offer appeal. They like a bargain, so if you have a "new limited" offer you can use this to re-engage.

5. Minimize their risk. Continue to follow up with references of others who are succeeding with your product/service. This makes them feel better about investing with you.

Compliant/Analytical follow-up

1. Manage the expectations. Be detailed with what they should expect from you along with specific timeframes. If something changes with the timeframe immediately make them aware of the changes.

2. Don't push. Maintain a reasonable follow-up process with very little pressure. They are very methodical when making a decision so plan for a longer response time than with a Driver or Influencer.

3. Create a tipping point. Making them aware of an upcoming price increase, change in the product line or lead time extension are reasons that might get them to return your call. However, do not pressure them as that will backfire!

4. Send additional information. Send something that can supplement the materials you gave them initially and use that as a follow up to make sure they received it and to answer any questions they may have.

Review this list whenever you are following up after an appointment. Knowing how to best approach a prospect based on their behavioral style may be the edge you need to get the return call!

DAY 86
Re-Ignite the Pain: Positioning Your Proposal

Eventually with persistent follow-up using the techniques covered in this book you will earn the right to present a proposal. In many cases your company will have specific details regarding how you are to put together a proposal. We are not talking about the physical proposal but rather the way you position the proposal.

Note: If your sales approach is to identify problems, raise the temperature and make a proposal on the same appointment. Then today's information would simply be included right after you've raised the temperature and confirmed with the prospect that you understand what they are looking for!

Too often salespeople jump to their proposal without taking the time to reinforce the results and challenges associated with the problems the prospect has shared in previous conversations. These salespeople assume the prospect is well aware of the importance of resolving their problem, after all, it's been weighing heavily on the salesperson's mind for some time! In many cases the prospect has a number of issues on their mind and this problem is just one of many. By taking a minute to bring the prospect back into *their world of the problem* with *all its challenges and pain* you increase their desire to respond positively to your solution.

Once you have your proposal put together take a few minutes to craft language around the following six steps so you are prepared to properly position your proposal.

Step 1. Identify their needs, wants and desires (problems). Depending on the behavioral style of the prospect you may want to speed up or methodically go through these details. Your goal is to bring them back to all the issues they initially shared with you.

Example 1 (service issue):

> "Kate, when we initially met you mentioned you wanted to improve the on-time delivery..."

Example 2 (product issue):

> "John, when we initially met you mentioned you wanted a larger screen on your computer..."

Step 2. Review the *pain* associated with each need, want or desire. You may want to use statements that include *their words, their issues* and *their stories* to help them quickly re-engage with the pain they shared. It's essential to review all of the issues and pain *before* you offer your solution in the form of the proposal.

Example 1 (service issue):

> "...you mentioned that delivery delays were causing a productivity drop. I wrote down you used the word "disaster" to describe a couple of recent episodes..."

Example 2 (product issue):

> "...you mentioned that your current screen was difficult on your eyes. I remember you said something about it being 'nearly impossible' when working with spreadsheets..."

Step 3. If you have quantifiable, measurable information now is the time to include that *before* you offer your solution.

Example 1 (service issue):

> "...you mentioned that it costs you about $3,000 every time the line goes down and that this occurs at least once a month..."

Example 2 (product issue):

> "...you mentioned you spend about $20 a day on coffee because of all the breaks you have to take..."

Note: If you had previously "obligated" the prospect during a previous sales appointment/in the letter of understanding with a statement such as "...and if we were able to come up with a solution to these problems you'd be willing to move forward?"...and they gave an affirmative response, then repeat that statement before you reach Step 4.

Example:

> "...and you mentioned that if we could come up with a solution to these problems you'd be willing to move forward."

Step 4. At this point you have sufficiently re-engaged the prospect with the issue, the pain and even the cost of the pain! You may have even reminded them of the subtle obligation they have made. They are *now* ready for your solution. *Now* you cover how your product/service will address this issue and relieve their pain!

Example 1 (service issue)

> "So, we included in our proposal a new method of guaranteed on-time delivery so you will always have your products on time and you will save at least $36,000 per year."

Example 2 (product issue):

> "So, we included a larger screen with a much higher resolution so you will be able to easily view your spreadsheets and you will save all that money you were spending on coffee."

Step 5. If the solution (this particular Feature) you are providing is a *unique competitive advantage* for your company then include that as part of positioning your proposal.

Example 1 (service issue):

"...we are the first and only provider to offer this level of guaranteed service in our industry..."

Example 2 (product issue):

"...we are the only manufacturer that can offer this size screen and resolution..."

While this may appear simple enough when reading the examples it is very difficult to do when you are in front of the customer and they are asking to see the bottom line on the proposal. Your desire to be "liked" may cause you to succumb to their request and immediately dump the proposal on the table and watch them flip to the page with the price. When they run to the price they typically forget all of their issues, all of their pain and all the costs associated with their current situation.

For today take out a proposal that you plan to present in the near future. Take the proposal through the five steps noted in this chapter. Write out the specific points as noted and run through it a few times before you go on the sales call. You're now ready to close!

DAY 87
Be Quick, Be Smart, Be Gone—
Closing Techniques For the Driver

Much has been written on the topic of closing. Unfortunately, many of the techniques are poor attempts to manipulate the prospect to do something they will regret as soon as they sign. Our approach is that *if* you've properly qualified the prospect, uncovered their issues and pain and provided a product/service that clearly addresses that issue and pain then with several trial closing techniques the prospect should become a customer and nearly close the sale for you! I use the word "nearly" as there are several ways to encourage the prospect to become a customer sooner rather than later.

The approach varies depending on the behavioral style of the prospect. If you recall from Day 2, the way *you* decide to buy may vary dramatically from the way *your prospect* buys.

Trial Closing – a fast word on a simple concept

A Trial Close is the incremental commitment you ask of your prospect on the way to closing the sale. Many of the techniques found in Days 87, 88, 89 and 92 are trial closing techniques. Trial closes may take place during the very first appointment. Questions such as "Is this what you were looking for?" "Have I answered your questions?" "What's the next step?" and "How does this look?" are small commitment questions that become a "trial close." The concept is the more commitments the prospect makes the more obligated they become and the closer they are to the sale. Often referred to as a "test close," you are testing the prospect's willingness to move forward with some incremental commitment. If the prospect responds negatively to your trial close then you know that you have some fast work to do before you can expect the sale to close.

Many of the questions we have already covered in this book are meant to encourage the prospect to make these incremental commitments. As noted above, if you use a number of trial closes during the course of the sales process *and your prospect responds with a commitment each time* you will the find the close to be less of an event and more of a simple step.

We will cover how to close the Driven/Dominant behavioral style today. The prospect with a Driven/Dominant behavioral style can pose a challenge. The Drivers' competitive and aggressive style may appear confrontational causing many salespeople to avoid asking for the order and they leave the appointment feeling dejected. However, with the proper approach the Driven/Dominant behavioral style can be closed quickly.

How to close a prospect with a Driven/Dominant behavioral style

Offer two to three alternatives – The Driver has a demanding and strong-willed style and will want to control your exchange. By offering them only one (1) option they are not so much in control as they are going along with what you've proposed. They may say "no" simply because they don't feel like they are making a good decision. If they have more than one option they get to make an informed decision, they get to choose and they are more in control. Too many options can be just as counterproductive as a single option so limit your options to 2-3.

They must "win" – The competitive nature of the Driver demands they win. This means you should be prepared to negotiate in the event they drive for a concession.

Ask their opinion – The Driver is often egocentric meaning what they say matters most! As a result you can use questions like "What way do you think is best?" when comparing the "two to three" options on your proposal. If you ask questions like "Do you like this?" in an effort to have others in the room hear the Driver's endorsement you are rolling the dice and the odds are not with you. The Driver likes to control and may say "no" just because they believe you are trying to direct them. If you ask the question "What way do you think is best?" and the Driver selects an option then others in the room are prone to listen to their selection and you achieve the same goal but without the risk.

Only offer suggestions when they ask. Drivers are often pioneering and venturesome, meaning they like to think outside the box. At the same time they want to control the exchange and the direction should ultimately come from their idea. They are prone to ask bigger questions aimed at pushing the envelope so be cautious with suggestions. When they ask for suggestions it is a positive sign. Finally, be careful to *only* offer ideas and suggestions that are currently available. If you share some "blue sky" thinking they may want to wait for the new improved idea you shared.

Close faster than normal and get out! – "Be Quick, Be Smart, Be Gone" may well be the motto of the Driver. Their demanding, aggressive and direct style often causes the salesperson to back off in order to avoid what they feel is a confrontation. This is a mistake. Their demanding, aggressive and direct style can mean a faster than normal close.

Ask for their direction – The Driver is often decisive and will move the sale forward if you just ask the question "What's the next step?" If the response is negative then you clearly know where you stand and you know it sooner rather than later (See Day 55).

Ask for their leadership – Ask "What would you like me to do?" or "What would you like me to do next?" Either of these questions asks them to lead you in the direction you should go. Also, their answer may position you to obtain an obligation from them. It may be appropriate after they answer the question to confirm "So, if I *am able to get you* XYZ then what's the next step after that?" Occasionally their next statement will be a clear direction and obligation on how to move the sale forward.

For today write a few of the statements you would ask and strategies you could use for your product or service from each of the ideas listed above. Identify a Prospect with a Driven behavioral style and use these techniques as soon as possible. Remember, practice makes permanent.

DAY 88
Stop the Fun: Closing Techniques for the Influencer

We will cover how to close the Social/Influencer behavioral style today. The Influencer's behavioral style can pose a problem because of the positive, friendly environment they create. The salesperson who desires to be "liked" does not want to introduce the confrontation of closing into this positive, friendly environment for fear of being disliked. However, there are several ways to approach the Influencer and achieve your goal of closing the sale and remaining a trusted sales professional.

How to close a prospect with an Influencer behavioral style

Reinforce their positive comments – Whenever the Influencer makes a positive comment about a feature, benefit or advantage of your product or service make sure to reinforce their insight. Reinforcing statements such as "That makes a lot of sense" or "I see what you're saying" will keep their optimism high and move them toward the close.

Good Deal! – The Influencer is often prompted to say "yes" when they feel like a good deal is on the table. They are frequently optimistic of your product and trusting of you and what you say about your product. Their tipping point might be the good deal you are offering them today. Keep the good deal in your pocket until you are ready to close.

Close abruptly – A sales call with the Influencer is typically a lot of fun. There's a lot of personal discussion, optimism and enthusiasm and making a commitment is not their primary concern. By abruptly closing with a statement like "So, are you ready to move on this?" or "So, do you want to place the order?" puts a temporary damper on the otherwise enjoyable discussion. The Influencer's desire to return to the enjoyable discussion typically gets them to answer in the affirmative. If they are not ready to go they will typically raise a key objection and then you can decide how to deal with the new objection. However, once you address the objection go right back with another abrupt close.

Watch out for buyer's remorse – Of all the different behavioral styles, the Influencer is the most likely to jump now and think later. As a result you will want to make sure you have them obligated beyond just their verbal confirmation. Having them authorize your paperwork or provide a down payment are two ways to ensure follow-through. Then, follow up in writing (e-mail, text message, letter, etc.) confirming the good decision they made and the positive "experience" they are about to enjoy.

Details, details, details – If you did not give them the detailed information as a "take-away" during or following the sale, then make sure to get it in their hands as soon as possible. Often there is another party involved with the purchase and that person may *not have an influencing behavioral style*. The other party may want to see the detailed information. When they begin to question the Influencer the sale may be put on hold or worse, cancelled. By providing the detailed information as a follow up and calling the Influencer's attention to the fact that you've given them the information "in case someone wants to see the particulars" you've decreased the probability of them backing out of the sale.

No sale? Follow up tenaciously – Of the four different behavioral styles the Influencer is the fastest to forget about your offer and get caught up in something completely different. When you have the Influencer and they are interested you need to close them if at all possible. If you *don't close* them then you must follow up often since the trail will go cold. However, they often re-engage the same way they lose interest…fast!

For today write a few of the statements you could make and strategies you could use for your product or service from each of the steps listed. Identify a prospect with an Influencing behavioral style and use these techniques as soon as possible. Remember, practice makes permanent!

DAY 89
"Steady as she goes"...Closing Techniques for the Steady/Amiable Behavioral Style

The closing approach for both the Steady/Amiable and the Compliant/Analytical styles are very similar. There are a few minor differences that are addressed these next two days but there are more similarities than there are differences.

Earlier we discussed the characteristics of a prospect with a Steady/Amiable behavioral style. We mentioned that they are the most difficult to identify because they have low emotion and a non-demonstrative behavioral style. The Influencer is talkative, optimistic and spontaneous (easier to identify). The Driver is impatient, direct, bottom line oriented (easier to identify). The Compliant is analytical, questioning, detail oriented (easier to identify). The Steady is, well, steady! This lack of excessive behavior carries over to the way they make decisions. They move deliberately and are very patient throughout the sales process. Depending on your behavioral style this may either line up perfectly with your approach *or* this will cause you anxiety as it takes much longer than you would expect. The techniques noted below will move the sale to a close as fast as possible.

How to close a prospect with a Steady/Amiable behavioral style

Begin by closing from the first appointment – The first time you meet you want to begin closing. The Steady will take longer than the other styles especially if your product or service is a change from what they are currently using! You will need to move the sale along using every approach mentioned in this section *on each call!* That's what we mean by closing from the first appointment.

Get incremental agreements throughout the sale – Right from the beginning you want to ask questions such as "How does that look?" or "Is this right?" or "Is this what you're looking for?" Don't expect a highly emotional confirmation! Simply getting them to agree and confirm what you shared with them looks good and will move the sale forward. They are very loyal and consistent. Even a simple agreement becomes an obligation later in the sale.

Take the Servant approach – When they respond affirmatively to your incremental agreements then ask them how you can serve them going forward. "What would you like me to do next?" or "What would you like to see next?" are great questions aimed at getting them comfortable with you so they will make the purchase. Credible comparisons – Be prepared to show how your solution is a bargain compared with your competition. *Do not* negative sell!

Share credible comparisons that are meant to show how your offer is the best value.

Don't push – Their relaxed, passive, deliberate approach to decisions requires that you also maintain a similar approach to the sale. You will sense their resistance to strong-arm tactics so avoid them at all costs. The extra patience and effort on your part will be repaid with a loyal, long-term customer. Their resistance to change will also work for you when a competitor comes knocking!

The "bargain" tipping point – The Steady appreciates a bargain so if you have a "limited" offer you can use this to re-engage and keep the sales process moving forward. Make sure your approach is passive and professional versus aggressive, forceful and cheap.

Don't run once you close! – When the Steady decides to purchase they are still in the decision making process. Confirm they've made the right decision by taking time to share with them how you will implement their order, installation, etc. After you thank them for their order and placing their confidence in you, take a few minutes to share the details of implementation. This will secure their confidence in you and their decision to buy from you.

Details, details, details – Given the fact that the Steady rarely gets into great detail, you may not have given them a lot of detailed information during the sale. Make sure to provide them the detailed information as a "take-away." Often there is another party involved with the purchase (could be someone who uses the product, created the specification or ultimately has to sign the check for your product/service) and they may *not be a Steady*. These other folks may want to see the detailed information and when they begin to question the Steady the sale may be put on hold, or worse, cancelled. By providing the detailed information as a follow up and calling the Steady's attention to the fact that you've given them the information "in case someone wants to see the particulars" you've decreased the probability of them backing out of the sale.

If you don't close:

Reasonable, consistent follow-up – If you did not get the order then share with them what you will do next so there are no surprises. Make the calls with low pressure, "Just checking in," "Want to make sure you have everything you need," "If you have any questions please feel free to give me a call" are examples of the approach that works. If they've shared with you they have a pressing date or timeframe then use this in the follow-up, "I want to make sure we hit the tight timeframe you shared with me..."

For today write a few of the statements you would ask and strategies you could use for your product or service from each of the steps listed above. Identify a prospect with a Steady behavioral style and use these techniques as soon as possible. Remember, practice makes permanent!

DAY 90
Sales Octane Mantra #25—When You Say "Yes" to Something You Say "No" to Something Else

One of the most difficult lessons for any salesperson to learn is to say "No." Our desire to be liked or appreciated by prospects and customers causes us to say "Yes" on a fairly regular basis. I'm not talking about the actual use of the word "no" but rather how we manage what we decide to do throughout the day. The reality is that we all have a limited number of hours every day; no one gets more or less than another. When we say "Yes" to something we have to say "No" to something else. We cannot give quality attention to more than one thing at a time. Even the best multi-tasking individuals have to make these decisions or their quality, productivity and ability to meet commitments will suffer.

On the other side of this dilemma is when we say "Yes" to something there are a host of other opportunities we have chosen to slam the door on. For instance, when we say "Yes" to a prospect that has to see us *"right away!"* we have decided to say "No" to:

1. the Prospecting calls we need to make
2. the Proposals we need to complete,
3. the Networking meetings we need to attend,
4. the Orders we need to enter,
5. the Customers we need to ask for referrals,
6. the Open Proposals we need to follow up on
7. and the list goes on!

All the other prior commitments receive a *No!* whenever we choose to say "Yes" to something else. You can't say "Yes" to everything and be successful in sales.

Unfortunately we seldom evaluate our commitments using this principle.

There are three essential steps we suggest you take on a daily basis to leverage this very important principle. This is not a book on time management; however, these steps will help you identify when to say "Yes" and when to say "No". Tomorrow we will discuss how to say "No."

1. Prioritize. I'm not talking about the traditional approach to prioritization with A's, B's, C's, A1, A2, etc. What I've found is that most salespeople have between one to ten things that must get done in a given work day. Take two minutes right now and identify the top ten (or less) items that you know you have to complete this coming Monday. Grab your planner or open the calendar on your Contact Management System and take a quick look to gather those top priority items. There are several items that should be on that list from our work to date; they include making prospecting calls, calling on open proposals and Expanding your Lead sharing group.

2. Next, take a look at the list and prioritize them (1-5). On Monday morning when you've checked your voice mail messages, instant messages, e-mail and other forms of communication you may want to update the short list based on new information (no more than ten).

3. Now, begin to execute on item #1. Stay on that top priority until a) you complete it (which will reinforce you and give you some serious energy), or b) you cannot do any more on the item most likely because you are waiting on a response from another party in order to continue forward. Do *not* go to the second, third or fourth item on your list until *a* or *b* has happened. When you say "Yes" to lower priorities, you say "No" to higher priorities. This is called procrastination or avoidance and it means you are saying "No" to your most important priorities!

During the day something will come up that you have to attend to because it is truly a new top priority. Perhaps a client calls and needs something immediately and you have to handle it right then and there. In this case you have a new top priority and you should focus on that new top priority until it is complete (*a* or *b*). Unfortunately, when we are interrupted by a more pressing need, once we finish dealing with that new top priority we seldom go back to the previous priority we were working on. We often run and complete a few easy items to help us feel good about our day. Meanwhile, the top priorities sit on our list, undone, and the pressure builds for the next day. When you use this process Monday, continue down the list of priorities until the day is done. Chances are you will seldom accomplish all the items on your list during the first several days or weeks you use this approach. This is because you have been saying "Yes" to a lot of simple items or because you are over-committed. After several weeks of using this process you will find you are completing more of your top priority items (including making prospecting calls, following up on orders, etc.) and your list will become more manageable. There's one more reason why this technique will help you improve your results. Studies show that when you are interrupted and move to a different task, even if only for several minutes, when you return to your original work it will take several more minutes just to get back to the same level of focus. This technique of staying on your priorities will improve your efficiency and effectiveness.

If you have numerous interruptions during the day from either internal team members or external prospects/customers you may have a challenge with managing expectations. We will address Managing Expectations tomorrow. For now write your *Top 5* list for Monday!

DAY 91
Sales Octane Mantra #26—
Managing Expectations: How to Say
"No"

It is difficult to say "No" especially when a prospect or customer is on the receiving end of the conversation. Our natural desire to be liked and not miss out on an opportunity often causes us to say "Yes" when we should have better managed the situation. There is a way to say "No" and still have the prospect or customer *like us*. There is a way to say "No" and secure the opportunity. As a matter of fact, your willingness to say "Yes" in an effort to be "liked" often results in just the opposite...being disliked. Think about it this way. If you say "Yes" to more than you can manage then someone you've already committed to (including yourself) is going to be disappointed with you for not meeting their expectation. The very thing we are trying to avoid, being disliked, is the very thing we get by saying "Yes" to everything.

The impact on teams when you over-commit

In many cases you have team members who support you that are the recipients of your over-commitments. When the prospect asks for the proposal or drawings the next day, and you say "Yes", in an effort to remain on their positive side, you may set yourself up to receive just the opposite. When we return to the office we tend to share the unreasonable request with the support staff wrapped in the flag of the customer to justify our commitment. "Well, the customer said they had to have it tomorrow and without their order we won't have a business very long"...sound familiar?

Three things happen at this point:

1. Our support staff loses confidence in the sales team. Barriers are erected and team work drops to a new "low." They look at you as if you are from another planet and you experience the very thing you are trying to avoid (being disliked).

2. The quality of the work decreases. The fact that the support staff has to complete the work in an unreasonable timeframe results in poor quality. The lower quality will reduce your opportunity with the sale and you experience the very thing you were trying to avoid (being disliked) when you initially said "Yes!"

3. Other customers lose. The support staff also has a limited number of hours in a day. They have other commitments that will not be met as a result of your over-commitment to another prospect. It may even be some of your customers! Once again, you experience the very thing you were trying to avoid when you initially said "Yes!" to the other prospect.

Take an intermediate step – Clarify!

If you are a typical sales professional you are an over-performer. You push hard, work hard and are goal oriented. You strive to go above and beyond and it's these very admirable traits that often cause you to over-commit. For instance, when a prospect says they need to see you ASAP (as soon as possible), your goal oriented approach is to say "Yes" and then figure out how to make it happen. In many cases the prospect may not need to meet with you for a few days.

Their idea of ASAP and your idea of ASAP may have been very different. By asking a clarifying question such as "ASAP meaning?" you get the prospect to provide some more information about the timeframe. Even if the prospect spells it out, "As soon as you can get over to this side of town!" you are now in control because it's as soon as *you* can get it. Manage the expectation! Don't simply say "Yes," ask clarifying questions to understand the prospect's sense of urgency.

In some cases the prospect simply asks for some information and our automatic response is to over-commit because we want them to "like us." Clarify by asking when they will review the information or when they would need to see the information. Most of the time their timeframe is well beyond what you were about to commit to! This allows you to get them the information *before* they expect it (now they like you more!) and it buys you valuable time to create a better response. Everyone wins.

Using the rules of Obligation & Reciprocity to get more commitment from prospects

Once you begin to manage expectations you can even create obligation on behalf of the prospect. When a prospect makes a request and you question them to clarify when they need it you can create obligation by asking for a commitment *before you agree*. For instance, think about the obligation buried in this statement.

"So, if I can get you the information by next Thursday... (thoughtfully pondering)...because I think I can move a couple of things around on my schedule...then you'll be able to let me know the next step by the following week?"

You can use your own scenario with this obligation approach. The key is to let them know that you will need to make an effort (schedule change, resource reallocation, etc.) to meet their timeframe, which creates obligation. Then, the rule of reciprocity kicks in which says that *if I do something for you* then you reciprocate and *you do something for me.*

What to do when the expectation is unreasonable – How to say NO

These are the most difficult to handle. In some cases your clarifying questions simply confirm that the prospect's expectation is unreasonable and you're going to have to choose your poison. If you over-commit then you know something else will have to suffer and you may not be able to provide a quality response to the prospect. On the other hand, you can share your concerns with the prospect, creating the impression that you are busy (other customers are buying from you!), your team is busy (your company is doing very well!) and that the deadline does not leave enough time for you to give them a quality response (quality and commitment are important to you and your company!). While you are saying "No, I can't do it", you are really putting the thought in their mind that customers are buying from you and your company because you do great work. In some cases the prospect will adjust their expectation because of what they hear and the way in which you have answered the question. If not, at least you have maintained your commitment to your customers and your competition will now over-commit! It's your choice.

Write the clarifying questions and obligation statement(s) on a notecard and keep them in the place where you typically get your incoming requests (office, car, computer screen, etc.). Begin to use them immediately *even if you have nothing on your calendar and can say "yes" to everything!* Get used to asking the clarifying questions and using obligation statements because before long you will arrive at a point where your calendar fills up!

DAY 92
"Details, Details"...Closing Techniques for the Compliant/Analytical Behavioral Style

As mentioned on Day 89, the closing approach for the Compliant/Analytical and Steady/Amiable styles are very similar. However, there are a few minor differences which we will cover today.

The Compliant/Analytical style is marked by their cautious, systematic and exacting approach to decisions. They are known for very thoughtful decisions having weighed all the evidence. The sales professional must approach the Compliant/Analytical with a careful, linear, accurate presentation in order to improve their probability of closing the sale. Depending on your behavioral style this approach may feel very foreign and slow. It's worth the extra effort since the Compliant/Analytical is a very loyal customer. They also make great referrals because everyone knows they do their homework. It's worth the effort!

How to close a Prospect with a Compliant/Analytical behavioral style

Start closing from the first appointment – The first time you meet you want to begin closing. The Compliant will take longer than the other styles especially if your product or service is a change from what they currently use or is unknown/untested. You will need to move the sale along using every approach mentioned in this section *on each call!* That's what we mean by closing from the first appointment.

Get incremental agreements; extreme version – Get incremental agreements throughout the sale. Right from the beginning you want to ask questions such as "How does that look?" or "Is this right?" or "Is this what you're looking for?" Don't expect a highly emotional confirmation! Simply getting them to agree and confirm that what you shared with them looks good and responds to what they are looking for will move the sale forward. The goal here is to get the Prospect talking. Whereas both the Steady and Compliant are more Introverted than Extroverted at least the Steady is more people oriented. The Compliant is all about tasks, details and analysis. You need to draw each test close response out of them by asking *extreme* questions such as "Have I given you *everything* you need?", "Is there *any* other information you need?" and "Have I answered *all* your questions about this feature?"

Use options – Similar to the Driver, the Compliant does not like to be painted into a corner. Therefore, giving them only one option feels a bit like they are in the corner and you'll notice them being evasive when you go for the close. By offering them two to three options you can identify which option they are leaning toward and move them closer to the sale.

Detailed Cost Justification – Be prepared to show how the product or service is "cost-justified." As you share the compelling analysis, use an incremental agreement trial close to make sure they are still tracking down the path toward a sale. If not, don't go into denial. Regroup, get the correct information and get back in front of them.

Listen to and *Watch* each response – Before asking for the order you want to be confident that you've given them what they asked for and have answered all their questions. If they respond to one of your incremental agreement questions with a half-committed "Well...yeah, I think so" the answer is a resounding *No!* Immediately confirm that it appears there is something else they might need. Don't go into denial. If they do not have all the information they need then when you ask for the order they will "want to get back to you" (code for "I'm going to have to keep looking"). You lose, they lose, everyone loses. Listen to and watch each response and adjust accordingly.

Share "the one downside..." – While not a frequently used approach this often works with extremely evasive and cautious prospects with a Compliant behavioral style. Because of their cautious nature they may be suspicious of your non-stop positive and optimistic statements about your product or service. If you have a "downside" that you know is not going to be a problem for them you can share it as "the one downside..." By offering the one downside you gain credibility because you're just like them, wanting to evaluate the pro's and con's! Again, only offer this if you know it is not going to be a problem in their situation.

Create a tipping point – If there's any deadline or time-sensitive consideration that might help to expedite the order then share that information in a non-confrontational manner. Tell them you want them to make sure you "deliver on time" or want to make sure they "take advantage of the discount", etc.

Do not push, let them direct you to the close – Ask the question "What's the next step?" and oftentimes they will tell you the specific step to close the sale. If they are not ready and want more information then identify how and when you will get the additional information to them and ask "Once I get that information to you what's the next step after that?"

Don't run once you close! – Similar to the Steady when the Compliant decides to purchase they are still in the decision making process. Confirm they've made the right decision by taking time to share with them how you will implement their order, installation, etc. After you thank them for their order and/or placing their confidence in you, take a few minutes to share the details of implementation. This will secure their confidence in you and your organization.

If you don't close:

Follow-up methodically – Maintain a reasonable and methodical follow-up process with very little pressure. Tell them when you are going to call again, why you are calling. For example: "Just want to follow up and see if you need additional information or have any more questions...I'll give you a call back next Thursday the 22nd."

For today write a few of the statements you would ask and strategies you could use for your product or service from each of the steps listed above. Identify a Prospect with a Compliant behavioral style and use these techniques as soon as possible. Remember, practice makes permanent!

DAY 92 Bonus
Always Send a Note of Thanks!

This can be e-mail, snail mail or gift mail but make certain you send a note of thanks! This simple act pairs you with a positive (Day 27 Sales Octane Mantra #7) and builds Obligation (Day 20 Sales Octane Mantra #5). This obligation is essential when you prepare to go back and ask for referrals! If you don't fashion yourself as a writer then here is the simple note: I really liked working with you. Thanks for your business/vote of confidence/support (choose one!).

Thank you!

Section 9: Referrals

DAY 93
Preparation for the Referral Meeting

The entire Sales Continuum process is built around bringing great value to your customers. During the sales process you have helped your customer uncover their real needs, you have raised the temperature of each need to the point where your customer sees all the issues, problems and challenges that result and what will happen if they don't take action. This brought them value! Furthermore, you created additional value by providing the right solution; one that addressed their real needs and helped them overcome or avoid the negative results they were experiencing. Finally, you went the extra mile to make sure everything went as planned and the solutions were implemented on time, as promised and you performed! With all that, you have earned the right to ask for and expect referrals.

You're ready to go for the secret of the Sales Continuum... referrals!

Step 1. List your recent installations (or those of your predecessor if you took over a territory).

Step 2. Identify the customer's initial criteria. If you followed the Sales Continuum process from the beginning you should have a paper trail of information around your customer's initial criteria. These are the issues or expectations they brought up as part of their buying criteria (Day 68, Question #4).

Step 3. Confirm that you did, in fact, meet or exceed each of the expectations. This is as simple as going down the list of criteria and putting a checkmark to confirm you met or exceeded the criteria. Feel free to write notes to help you remember certain stories or references that will reinforce to the customer that you did a great job. These may include a comment made by the customer about a particular feature, or something positive the customer mentioned about the installation, etc.

Step 4. If you failed to meet a particular criterion you have two options: 1) If you can still fix the situation then do it immediately. You maximize your opportunity to secure referrals when you meet or exceed your customer's expectations. 2) If the sale is completed and there's nothing you can do, recognize that it may come up when you ask for referrals so be prepared to deal with the issue if they bring it up! At least you're prepared.

Step 5. Make note of any extra efforts you made to accommodate your customer. In many cases your customer will make a last minute change, be unable to receive the product when initially planned, increase or decrease the quantity making it difficult for you or miss a date on their end of the agreement and your team went above and beyond to accommodate. In each of these cases you want to have this information ready when you go in to ask for referrals. In effect your customer "owes" you for these changes/errors and in most cases you did not receive anything more than a "thanks for helping me out." Now is the time to get something for your extra effort and it comes in the form of a referral.

Note: it is not appropriate to call attention to a mistake/error made by your customer since you pair yourself with a negative. Take a few minutes and develop a question or two for each of the ways you went above and beyond that will get the customer to recognize your efforts. For instance, if the client changed the installation date then rather than say "Sally, remember when *you had to change* the delivery date...and we were able to accommodate the change, how did that work?" (which is negative), instead ask, "Sally, regarding the delivery timeframe, we started out with the 15th of January and then we moved that out to the 30th, how did that work for you?" In most cases, when you ask a question in this manner the customer will pick up on the situation, and, then reinforce you for doing a great job accommodating their change to the date, etc.

Step 6. Develop questions that will prompt the client to either complete the question or confirm that you met or exceeded their expectations. For instance, if one of the initial criterion was "stay within our budget", and you know you were able to deliver on that, then write the question "Sally, when we started the project it was important that we stayed within your budget, right? (Sally responds, "yes"). And how did we do on that requirement? (Sally responds, "Great!")."

Occasionally your customer will have an employee who makes a very positive statement to you about your product/company, etc. Keep that information written down for this moment. There's nothing better than to make a statement "Sally, last week John Jones mentioned to me that the new software was really working well...is that what you're hearing?" While this may seem like a lot of preparation, recognize that you will use the same questioning process regardless of the customer. The only thing that will change is the situation (budget, specific criteria, timeframe, and so forth). The key is to have questions that will engage the customer in the process so the customer voices the benefits you have brought them, the ways you went above and beyond for them and the accolades of their employees regarding your product. When you finally get in front of the customer using this process you will use these questions and process to engage your client so the positives come rushing forward! Those positives create a presumption of obligation. The customer will have the presumption they are obligated to you for the hard work you've done. You, in turn, are going to leverage their obligation by requesting referrals. Remember, and this is key, no obligation...no referrals. Follow the steps and you'll be blessed with referrals!

For today go back and look at your installations over the past 93 days. Compile a list of all your installations and the steps from today's material and you're ready to go for the secret of the Sales Continuum — referrals!

DAY 94
Getting the Referral Appointment

Now that you are armed with your preparation from Day 93 it's time to get the appointment to ask for referrals. While you can certainly ask for referrals any time throughout the sales process, we are focusing our efforts at the end of the process when you can leverage your hard work and obligate them to share referrals. And while asking for referrals over the phone will work, seeing the customer face to face typically generates a better result.

There are a number of reasons you can use to secure the referral request appointment. The typical request is to meet with the customer to "close out the order/project/sale." The reason might be:

- To drop off the warranty/receipt/instructions for the product or service they purchased.

- To take an "after" photo for the "before/after" scenario. Remember Day 53 and the importance of getting "before" pictures for subsequent marketing and prospecting? Now is the time to get the "after" photo. The good news about this option is the timing will typically fall soon after the completion of the project so the product will still look good!

- To complete the customer satisfaction survey and you need to do it in person. If you are not using some sort of survey following the sale you need to implement this as soon as possible. This provides you with insight for future product/service improvements *and* positions you beautifully for the referral (especially if you include the following question in your survey "Would you recommend us to a friend/business colleague?").

- Drop off a gift of thanks. Given the size of the sale and the resulting commission, you might want to drop off a gift.

- Complete a final walk-thru. If your product/service demands a final "punch-out" you may want to use this as your reason to meet and "close out the sale." One note of caution. If you have significant issues that surface during the "walk-thru" you should hold off on asking for referrals until the issues have been resolved.

- A "30/60/90-day check-up" – This technique is wonderful if you get busy and a few months slip by after the installation is complete. Give your customer a call and tell them you want to do a 90 day check-up on how the product/service is working. Make this your policy!

- Last, but not least, if you can't use any of the aforementioned techniques tell them you "want to stop by to make sure we're all set." Be careful with this option as the customer may be very satisfied and will say there's no reason for you to stop by since everything is perfect. They are saying this because they don't want to inconvenience you. The problem is, you don't get your referrals. You can always say "it's our company policy" that you need to stop by and close out the paperwork.

Don't accept no for an answer!

Note: It's best to schedule this appointment soon after the product is delivered or the service has been received. The more time that passes the greater the probability they will not be as excited about the new product or the service you completed for them. It's like buying a new car. You're really excited when you first get it but when the payment book arrives, the newness wears off and the larger insurance bill arrives you are not quite as excited as you were initially. Make the call soon!

DAY 95
Asking for a Referral

Now you are ready for the referral appointment.

Step 1. Complete whatever it was that you used as the reason for the appointment: photo, dropping off a gift, completing the survey, covering the warranty, etc.

Step 2. Say that you want to "close out" the project/order/ paperwork and find a place to sit down (hold the paperwork to make it apparent you need to sit down).

Step 3. Go through the list of their initial criteria points and ask confirmation questions to confirm that you met each criterion.

Example:

> You: Sally, I just want to confirm we did a good job, up front. You wanted to make sure we did (criterion). How did that work out?
>
> Sally: Great!
>
> You: You also wanted to (criterion), how did that turn out?
>
> Sally: That worked out just fine.

When you are done with the list of criteria segue into any possible things that you did above and beyond to accommodate their changes, errors, etc.

Example:

> "Oh, now the change in the installation date when the flooring contractor got behind...how did we do to accommodate that change?"

Step 4. Tug for the heart. As soon as you have completed how your company has met or exceeded the customers expectations then segue with a tug of their heart. For example: "You know, I've really enjoyed working on this project with you."

Step 5. *Ask for the referral!* "One of the ways I build my business is through referrals. Who can you think of that might benefit from the same results you received?"

Step 6. Now sit there and wait. Don't talk. The minute you talk you interrupt their thought process. The reason they are quiet is they are truly trying to think of whom they might be able to refer you to. In some cases they may be able to remember one or two possible referrals. More often than not they will respond with "I really can't think of anyone right now but leave me some of your cards and when I think of someone I'll give them a card." I'll lay odds that your cards will sit around for a few weeks and eventually find their way to the circular file (trash bin). Don't let them off the hook!

The reason that customers have such a difficult time thinking of possible referrals is two-fold. First, they are not sure of what you're looking for. Second your request is too broad and they can't see their friends or colleagues that may be an ideal referral.

To help them overcome these issues you need to review the information you developed on Day 30, Step 1 for the Wheel of the Fortunate. During that step you identified the conditions that exist when someone needs your product or service. Take that list of conditions and read on. You now want to help them see the faces of their friends and colleagues. On Day 60 you learned about identifying what "circles" your customer runs in. You'll need to have that list of associations, committees, clubs, organizations, boards, sports organizations, religious organizations, non-profit entities, etc., with you before you have your appointment to ask for referrals.

Step 7. Here's what combining the conditions and the circles they run in sounds like:

"Gail, oftentimes organizations that are moving or planning to move can benefit from our product/service. I know you're on the education committee for the Clinical Laboratory Managers Association. Who can you think of at the CLMA that might be moving or planning to move in the future?"

That's it. What you've done is painted a very *visual* picture of what and who you *want them to* "*see.*" When you paint this visual picture they will "see" in their mind many of the members at their CLMA meetings.

Second, they have a condition to remind them of what to look for.

Finally, after they can't "see" any additional referrals thank them for the names and then ask them for all the details!

- Correct spelling of the referral's name, company, name, and the like.

- Referral's contact information, telephone number, e-mail, etc.

- If they have not already given you information as to why they thought of the referral then ask the question "Why did you think of Bob Jones?" This will be helpful information when you begin prospecting Bob Jones. It's the "reason" you will use when you make your prospecting call to Bob Jones!

- Ask your customer if they would be willing to make a call to the referral to introduce you. For example, "Gail, would you be willing to make an introduction for me to Bob?" If they are unwilling to make an introduction, usually because they are not that close with the person, then make sure you ask them the next step.

- Ask if you can use their name as a reference. For example, "Gail, can I use your name as a reference when I call Bob?" Almost 100 percent of the time they will agree to let you use their name and that's all you really need to create the environment to secure an appointment.

- That's it! Now you have a few referrals to put into the Sales Continuum beginning with the material from Day 37.

For today prepare the information for Steps 1–7 and *write out the talking points* so you are confident when asking for referrals! The better you help the Customer visualize groups of people (the circles they run in) and the conditions when someone might need your product or service the easier it becomes to obtain referrals.

DAY 96
Rewarding the Referrer

When you give you receive. That's not the reason we should give but the principle still works. When someone gives you a referral they improve your opportunity to sell. As noted earlier, referrals are the secret of sales success. You owe the person who gives you a referral.

At the same time, the principle of reinforcement comes into play; whatever you reinforce you get more of. You want others to continue to give you referrals so if you reinforce them with a reward they are inclined to give you more. Not only do you owe them for the referral, you want to reward them because it will motivate them to give you additional referrals!

When should you reward them?

You typically reward someone for a referral when the referral has resulted in a sale or after you have been paid. You *may* bait them with a commitment to *make it worth their while*, but you reward them when it becomes a sale! If you reward them when they give you the referral then they are going to expect to be rewarded with each referral regardless of the outcome. When a particular referral does not result in a sale it's difficult to "renegotiate." By waiting to reward them after the sale you keep them engaged during the entire sales process.

Once the sale has been completed or the invoice has been paid in full you want to be diligent in following through with the reward. Once you set the expectation and begin rewarding someone for a referral you will notice how they often keep track of the sale. If you get busy, or worse, greedy, and fail to reward them you will not only shut off the flow of referrals but also "pair" yourself with a negative! (S/he did not follow through!)

What should you use as a reward?

What you use as a reward often becomes a significant point of discussion. The first choice is whether to use money or gifts. Money is only the best option if the person giving you the referral has specifically stated they want to be paid for the referral (and you have agreed), or if you know that money will truly motivate them to give you more referrals. Write the check and watch the flow of additional referrals. These situations are becoming less frequent due to conflict of interest.

The second choice is a gift. If you've not agreed to pay cash or if the person is not likely to be excited about a financial reward then a gift is the best reward. What type of gift is important? You want to provide them with gifts that will pass three tests:

- It's experiential.

- It involves something emotional.

- It engages another person (not you).

Experiential – Give them something they get to experience. Reward them with a gift card for a dinner to their favorite restaurant. Reward them with a day at a SPA. Give them a certificate for golf at an exclusive club. The key is to give them a reward they will *experience.*

Emotional – Reward them with several tickets for their favorite sports team. Reward them with a purse from their favorite designer. Reward them with sports memorabilia from their hero. Reward them with something that stirs up emotion and you pair yourself with that positive emotion.

Involves another person (not you) – Picture this: you reward someone with a gift certificate to their favorite restaurant. Better yet, you made some calls and found out their spouse or significant other's favorite restaurant. Toward the end of dinner the bill comes, the gift card goes down and the other person asks the question "Who gave you the gift card?" They answer it came from you which begs the question "Why?" They explain you gave them the gift card in appreciation of a referral. The next statement from the other person will be something along the line of "Give them *more* referrals!"

Many times during our workshops salespeople will ask whether taking someone to a sporting event is an appropriate way of rewarding them for a lead. Our response is usually NO. If you are there, with them, then it's eventually going to result in a discussion of business and that's not a reward. If you gave them 2-4 tickets so they could take their spouse or significant other/kids/another couple, *and* you're not with them...it's a good gift.

How should you position the reward?

Be sure to pair the reward with the reason for the reward. Send a note and share with them that you appreciated the connection they made and that it ultimately resulted in a sale. Thank them for their help.

Now you've tied the reward with the reason for the reward and you've made it personal and emotional. Be prepared to receive other referrals!

Two things to avoid with referral rewards

Don't follow up. Don't make a call a few days after the sporting event or a few weeks after you sent them the gift certificate to see how they enjoyed their time out. This appears that you are making the call to see if they have other leads. Let it go! When you give you receive. Let the principle work!

Don't stop. There's a tendency to stop rewarding after a while, especially if you are getting a lot of leads from a particular person. As soon as you stop rewarding then you are reinforcing that you don't care about leads. Don't forget that without their lead you would not have the sale or the commission in the first place! When you give you receive so *keep giving!*

Take time today to identify the appropriate reward for recent referrals.

You've now come full circle with the Sales Continuum. You started 96 days ago and you've finished with referrals. The new referrals you receive will go directly into your Prospecting process and you will begin to see your sales grow faster and your client base grow larger.

DAY 97
Sales Octane Mantra #27—Perfect Practice Makes Perfect and Permanent

The old adage "Practice Makes Perfect" is not correct. Just watch any golfer at the driving range and you will quickly agree that many of them are either there for the first time in their life or they just keep practicing the same incorrect mechanical swing and same poor habits. By continuing to go to the driving range and hitting one bucket after another they are permanently reinforcing the same incorrect mechanical flaws which will deliver the same poor result. Practice does not make perfect, practice makes permanent! Perfect practice makes perfect. Athletes refer to this perfect practice as building muscle memory, or its scientific name "motor memory." Basically the professional athlete practices the same perfect move over and over again until they make the move without consciously thinking about it. The muscles and brain work together to literally remember each move as they go through the motion so they can do it with little conscious effort. This state is often referred to as being "in the zone." When you go on a sales call and begin to ask questions, answer questions and share information about your product or service you are using the "motor skill" known as speech. To the extent that you practice what you are going to say you build the same "motor memory" a professional athlete uses to make that great move.

If you consistently practice the techniques in this book you will build the motor memory to excel when you are in the moment. As questions and objections fly at you it's not a problem because you have practiced the responses and are in the zone.

Too often we start thinking about what we are going to say just a few minutes before we make a phone call or walk into an appointment. When the prospect responds with an objection or asks a question we wing it. This "last minute approach" is reinforced by the fact that seldom, if ever, are we asked to leave the prospect's office because our response was not perfect. Many salespeople continue in a world of imperfection much like many of the golfers at the driving range because no one shows them a better way. The sales professional takes a different approach. They practice their perfect objection responses, they practice the perfect product demonstration, they practice the perfect presentation, they practice the perfect cold call, they practice the perfect voicemail response. In the process of consistently practicing the perfect approach they build the motor memory. These same sales professionals become identified in their industry with words such as "smooth," "articulate," "professional," and "top performer." They were just like you when they first decided on a career in sales. But they practiced with perfect material and before long they were in the zone! Perfect practice makes perfect and permanent. Make it a point today to plan time each week to have that practice...perfect!

DAY 98
Sales Octane Mantra #28—It's Not How You Start It's How You Finish

Regardless of your current situation it's only that, your current situation. Some of you have made incredible progress with the Sales Continuum process during the previous 97 days. Some of you may have started the Sales Continuum process and run into challenges, obstacles or interruptions. You started with the best of intentions but were sidetracked. The key is to determine how you will get back on track and achieve your goals!

Several years ago I decided to take up running. There is no shortage of running accessories and I invested in all of them. The running shoes, running clothes, running outerwear, running socks, running sunglasses, running gloves for the cooler weather and running earphones for the running digital audio players. Next there were running books and training manuals meant to coach me in the right direction. Finally, there was equipment—tread mills and exercise bicycles to round out my training. I invested in all of them because I was committed to running!

None of this prepared me for the reality of how I felt once I actually started running. It was not as easy as the books, videos and instruction manuals made it look. All the equipment improved my situation; however, running required a lot more effort and pain than I had expected. There are several things I learned quickly.

1. When I ran I found that setting incremental goals while running made it easier to achieve my final destination. Picking a landmark half a mile down the road and running to that goal was manageable. Upon meeting that incremental goal I would select another landmark another half mile down

the road. It was easier to achieve the incremental goals along the way than to look three miles down the road.

2. When I stopped I found it very difficult to re-start. Once I stopped short of my goal it was very difficult to get started running again. Much of this was mental. It was as if I had given up. Then my physical side would remind me of how nice it was to walk and be able to breathe normally. It was a false sense of satisfaction as I was no longer achieving my goal.

3. During subsequent runs I found I was prone to stop more often because I stopped during the last run. My lack of achievement reinforced my inability to get to the next level. Even when I finally finished the run there was something missing because I had stopped along the way.

4. If I set my mind to completing the run, without stopping, and persevered through the mental and physical assaults, I had a much greater sense of accomplishment and subsequent runs became less difficult. The reinforcement that came with finishing the run and achieving my goal had positive implications far beyond simply running.

Set incremental goals as you move forward! If you made incredible progress during the past 97 days then continue forward and set new incremental goals to continue to grow your sales. If you ran into challenges, obstacles or interruptions that kept you from achieving your goals then pick up where you left off and set incremental goals to help you get back on track.

Keep going! Recognize that every time you stop it is much more difficult to get back on track. Status quo is not possible with human development. You are either moving forward or going in reverse. When you keep moving forward you are moving in the right direction. Once you start, keep going. It's the only way to reach the finish line!

When you accomplish a goal reinforce yourself! By reinforcing your accomplishment you increase the probability of succeeding in similar endeavors in the future. Whatever you reinforce you get more of so reinforce your incremental accomplishments and you'll begin to attract even greater success!

Take time today to reinforce the accomplishments you've already made and make:

- The commitment to set incremental goals going forward!

- The commitment to keep going regardless of the challenges!

- The commitment to continually reinforce yourself with each accomplishment!

DAY 99
Is Sales the Right Role for You?

The question is often asked, "How long should it take before I know whether a new salesperson is going to make it?" It's not a trick question. Sales managers wonder how long it should take before they know whether a new salesperson is going to make it or whether they should move on. It's a good question.

The answer is, "It depends, but certainly no longer than 100 days." That's not a trick answer. Regardless of the sales cycle for your product or service, when a salesperson has a clear plan for the incremental steps in their sales process and diligently completes the steps as set forth in the plan, that is a very good indication of how well they will do long term. The only variable is the amount of time spent on product training (i.e. If you have a 6 week product training schedule before you enter the field then the "100 day clock" starts at the end of the product training).

There are two key caveats: the plan/strategy for the salesperson and the follow through by the salesperson. When a company brings on a new salesperson the company must have a clear plan and strategy to help make that salesperson become successful. That's why this book was written. It's a template that a company can use to clearly measure whether the new salesperson is doing all the activities and evaluate whether the new salesperson has developed the sales skills to be successful! If you are self-employed or if your new employer does not have a clear plan/strategy to help you become successful then it's up to you to develop the plan! Aside from the specific number of calls, proposals or sales you must make, this book will provide you with a comprehensive plan for the first 100 days *and beyond!*

The second caveat is the follow through by the sales person. And that's why on Day 99 we are posing the question *"Is sales the right role for you?"* Be honest, how have you done over the past 98 days? Have you learned the techniques, followed the process and been diligent about meeting your measurable goals? Have you had success when Networking? Have you had success diligently?

Prospecting? Have you uncovered qualified opportunities? Have you developed and asked great questions when on a call? Have you moved the opportunity to the next step? Have you successfully closed sales? Have you gone back and asked for Referrals? *Is sales the right role for you?*

Ultimately it does not matter what your employer thinks. . . it's your decision. If you believe sales is the right role for you then you have the right attitude to become a sales professional. For today look back over the past 98 days at where you had success, identify your sales strengths and write them down. Look back over the past 98 days and where you fell short and write down your areas for improvement. Tomorrow you will sit down with your sales manager or, if self-employed, an accountability partner and plan the future!

DAY 100
Setting a Positive Course For the Future!

Yesterday we mentioned that sales managers often ask, "How long should it take before I know whether the new salesperson is going to make it?" Today you're going to be proactive and answer the question for your sales manager. Even if you have been in sales for many years with your company you owe it to yourself to take this step with your sales manager!

It's best to make mid-course corrections sooner rather than later before your challenges will become bad habits. It's been roughly three months since you started this process. Yesterday you wrote your list of successes and your strengths. You also wrote down your challenges and the areas where you need to improve. Now it's time to sit down with your sales manager and share your findings. If sales is the right role for you then now is the time to get their commitment to your continued success! Here are the items to cover:

The sales manager's expectations – Whatever plan you were given or expectations that were placed upon you when you started should be reviewed.

Your results – Review your progress with regard to the plans and expectations given to you by your sales manager. This begins to build their confidence in your abilities!

Your recent effort – Share the work you have done over the past 100 days with the techniques, processes and skills in the book. This reinforces you are a self-motivated and self-disciplined sales professional!

Your strengths and how to leverage – Review your list of strengths and ask them whether they agree with your observations. Dig and probe to make sure you are in agreement. Now spend a few minutes talking about how best to leverage your strengths going forward. This informs your sales manager of your strengths and builds their confidence in your value to the sales team.

Your areas for improvement and how to address – Review your list of challenges and the areas of improvement you've identified. Ask them whether they agree with your observations. Dig and probe to make sure you are in agreement. Identify several options for how to improve in each area where you need to improve. This shows your sales manager you are self-aware of your challenges *and* you are actively working to improve in those areas!

Go forward plan and timeframe – Finally, do not leave without a plan and a timeframe. Here are a few tips to use during this step so your plans/goals will help you succeed.

- Make certain whatever you agree with is clearly understood by both you and your sales manager.

- Make certain each item can be measured. Ask yourself the question "How will I know I have met this expectation?"

- Is this goal reasonable? Has anyone ever attained this before? Would your sales manager be willing to agree to this goal if they were in your position?

- Will the achievement of this goal make a difference to your sales? Set plans that drive sales volume.

- There needs to be a date when each agreed upon step in the plan will be completed.

Now you have support from your sales manager and a clear plan to continue your success. Congratulations! You're on your way to becoming a sales professional!

Dedications

To my wife, the best friend I have. Thank you for putting up with my bottomless energy, laser-like drive and constant activity. You're the best!

To my Children: Katherine, Ryan, Elizabeth and Anna. I learn from you every day. Continue doing what you love and a wonderful life will follow.

To my Father who taught me the discipline of Integrity and Hard Work and my Mother who was always optimistic! Three principles required for sales success.

To my Creator, God, who has given me everything I have including the gift to enjoy this race called life

Diane Lee Photography

Jim Ryerson is the founder and president of Sales Octane, Inc., a group of individuals dedicated to helping others apply time- honored sales principles to grow themselves and their business. Jim started his selling career with Herman Miller, Inc., one of America's most admired corporations. Ranked as one of the top 25 sales forces in the country by Sales and Marketing Magazine, Jim developed several selling models during his time with Herman Miller, Inc.

29991613R00154

Made in the USA
Middletown, DE
09 March 2016